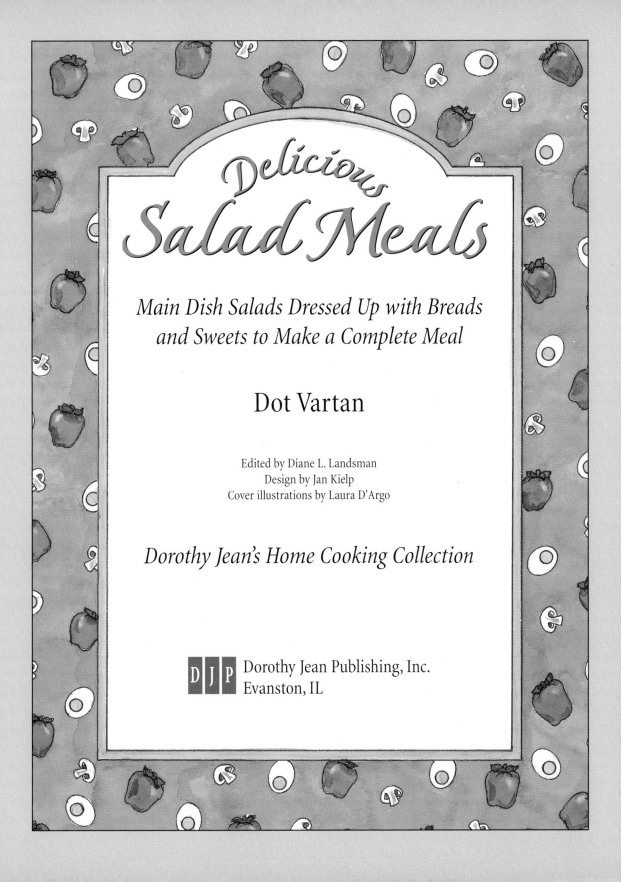

Delicious Salad Meals

Main Dish Salads Dressed Up with Breads and Sweets to Make a Complete Meal

Dot Vartan

Edited by Diane L. Landsman
Design by Jan Kielp
Cover illustrations by Laura D'Argo

Dorothy Jean's Home Cooking Collection

DJP Dorothy Jean Publishing, Inc.
Evanston, IL

Acknowledgments

To my husband Gentre, thanks for your ongoing support of my publishing ventures. Thanks also to Teri Montante for helping me test the recipes.

Edited by Diane L. Landsman
Designed by Jan Kielp, jmkdesign, ltd.
Cover illustrations by Laura D'Argo
Proofread by Melissa Stehlik
Index by Elizabeth A. Matlin

Dorothy Jean Publishing, Inc.
62 Williamsburg Road
Evanston, IL 60203
SAN #256-0151

ISBN 1-884627-11-0
Library of Congress Catalog Control Number: 2004097124

Library of Congress Cataloging-in-Publication Data
Available from the Library of Congress

Printed in the U.S.A.
10 9 8 7 6 5 4 3 2 1

Other books by Dot Vartan:
Delicious Fruit Desserts
Mad About Muffins
Is It Soup Yet?

A Bounty of Delicious Salads— and More

Writing a cookbook is a series of discoveries. One of my first discoveries while researching this book was the similarity between soups and salads. While one is served hot and the other cold, they both embody a variety of ingredients and flavors, allowing you to make creative substitutions with successful results. In addition, they both can be reasonably fast to prepare and are comfort foods.

Salad is a comfort food? You bet! Even though they are often viewed as healthy (loaded with vegetables, low in carbohydrates and fat), salads can also summon pleasant food memories, just like soup. Remember Mom's creamy tuna salad for lunch? Or her golden yellow egg salad that was so good you didn't mind that it was made with leftover dyed Easter eggs? Doesn't a summer barbecue seem incomplete without Aunt Sally's garden potato salad or Grandma's rainbow fruit salad?

Even if your idea of comfort food is sipping a steaming bowl of chicken soup to soothe a cold, salads are just as comfortable and easy to enjoy. Simply take some of your favorite ingredients, toss them with greens, pasta, or grains, splash on a little dressing and voilà—you have a quick, satisfying dish.

It's time to elevate salads to the next level by transforming them into satisfying entrées. With this recipe collection, you'll learn how to create main-dish salads with the pork tenderloin, fish fillets, sirloin steak, or chicken breasts that you often grill. Simply add an aromatic rub, tangy homemade dressing, and fresh fruits and vegetables then serve over crisp greens. Have you ever substituted napa cabbage for lettuce? How about pairing juicy melon with chicken, or smoked salmon with mangoes? And when was the last time you enjoyed a *halibut* cobb salad? *Delicious Salad Meals* takes you on a journey that transforms main-dish salads from comfortable food to memorable meals. There are sublime salads elegant enough to serve at an intimate dinner party and portable salads to pack and tote to sporting events or picnics. And if you're in a meatless mood, there's a chapter devoted to hearty salads composed of vegetables, fruits, grains, pasta, cheese, and eggs.

Even though "salad as the main event" is the focus of this book, I couldn't forget about Aunt Sally's garden potato salad. Popular side salads are included in the Salad Parties chapter, which provides recipes for such festive gatherings as a backyard barbecue, potluck supper, and weekend brunch. When guests ask what they can bring to your party, simply send them one of the recipes from the menu. And to make your meal planning even easier, I've created complete menus to accompany every salad meal. There are breads, muffins, biscuits, rolls, tarts, and desserts, too. All you have to do is make the grocery list, shop, and get cooking!

When you're out shopping, be sure to explore produce stands and seasonal farmers' markets for a larger selection of fresh ingredients. Fresh herbs infuse salads and dressings with great flavor, so experiment with your favorites. Rather than purchasing small, expensive packages of fresh herbs at the supermarket, look for large bunches of reasonably priced fresh herbs at small, local markets.

Remember those creative substitutions I said were easy to make? Feel free to adapt these recipes to suit your tastes. Incorporating leftovers into a salad is a great way to experiment with flavors and use up small portions of vegetables, dried fruits, olives, rice, pasta, or deli meats.

I urge you to become comfortable with making the vinaigrettes and creamy dressings included with the salads. They truly are quick and easy to prepare once you get into the habit of making them. And while much more flavorful than bottled dressings, they won't mask the taste of the other ingredients. Be sure to read through the introduction for helpful information and tips on preparing salads and dressings.

I hope you enjoy my salad meals and embark on a journey to discover your own!

Dot Vartan
June, 2005

Helpful Recipe Tips

- Large eggs were used for these recipes.

- For certain fresh fruits and vegetables—such as pears, mangoes and avocados—it is best to have more on hand than the recipe calls for in case they are overripe or spoiled.

- Be sure to visit produce stands, as well as seasonal farmers' markets, for a good selection of the freshest fruits and vegetables. The quality of these ingredients is especially important in salads.

- Always dress salads just prior to serving them—and go easy on the dressing. It is meant to be a sauce for the salad. It should complement, rather than mask, the flavors of the ingredients.

- A colander and a salad spinner help make the preparation work much easier.

- Learn knife skills in order to chop vegetables more quickly. Chopped or sliced vegetables that are uniform in size are more visually appealing, they cook evenly, and they are easier to eat.

Table of Contents

Introduction

Salads began as simple fare— seasoned greens and herbs—and were usually served as a first course or side dish. The salad-as-a-meal concept began with the cobb salad, which was created in 1936 at the Brown Derby restaurant in California. Named for its creator, Robert Cobb, it was the precursor of today's composed salads. Generous amounts of greens were combined with small amounts of bacon, blue cheese, turkey, and avocado to create a satisfying meal. It became very popular with celebrities who were conscious of their waistlines. Today, main-dish salads are a mainstay on restaurant menus and prepared frequently at home for lunch or dinner.

Lettuces and Greens

There are hundreds of lettuce varieties that can be used for salad making and they all fall into four general categories:

Iceberg: Also known as crisphead, iceberg lettuce has a firm, compact, pale-green head and very mild flavor due to its high water content. Because it's sturdy and versatile, iceberg is the lettuce of choice for most fast food restaurants and food service markets.

Romaine: Named for the Greek island where it originated, Cos or romaine lettuce has a crisp, crunchy texture and is best known for its use in Caesar salad. The whitish leaves closest to the core are the most flavorful part of the head.

Tips for Preparing Salad Greens

- Buy the freshest greens with crisp leaves that are free of brown spots.

- Use greens as soon as possible after purchasing. When storing, remove any wilted leaves and rubber or metal bands and place in a perforated plastic bag. Store greens in the refrigerator's vegetable bin.

- Always wash greens. Some greens, particularly spinach, are notoriously sandy and need several washings to remove all the grit. The easiest way to wash greens is to separate the leaves and place them in a clean sink full of cold water. Gently swish them around the water and then remove them to dry. Generally, the dirt will fall to the bottom of the sink as the leaves float to the top.

- For drying, salad spinners make the work much easier. Or, gently press the leaves between clean kitchen cloth or paper towels. Always dry greens after washing them since dressing clings better to dry leaves.

- Once they are washed and dried, refrigerate greens as whole, untorn leaves until you are ready to use them.

- When you are ready to make the salad, tear the greens by hand into smaller pieces. Crisp greens can be sliced or shredded with a knife.

- Always add the dressing just before serving to prevent the greens from wilting.

Butterhead: Tender and delicately flavored, butterhead lettuce has tiny, sweet inner leaves at its heart and progressively larger, soft leaves toward the outside. Familiar varieties include Bibb, Boston, butter, limestone, and red tip. Its sweet, buttery flavor combines well with stronger-flavored greens. Served alone, butterhead lettuce is best tossed with a light-flavored dressing that highlights its soft texture.

Looseleaf: Tender and mild, these lettuces do not form into heads. Their leaves are generally curly and large and range in color from medium to dark green with some being red-tipped. The many varieties include red leaf, green leaf, Ruby and oak leaf.

In addition to lettuce, there are many greens used in salad making. While spinach and cabbage can be served alone, others are usually mixed with lettuce to provide flavor and texture accents.

Spinach: A perennial favorite, spinach is sold loose, tied in bunches. It can also be found prewashed and packaged in bags. Baby spinach has very small leaves and is milder in taste.

Cabbage: Green and red cabbages, savoy, and Chinese or napa cabbage are all crisp greens that are usually shredded and used frequently in side salads.

Chicory: Another category of leafy plants, chicory includes such varieties as Belgian endive, curly endive, escarole, and radicchio. These greens add texture and variety to salads. Their slight bitterness is a nice complement to sweet and sour flavors.

Arugula and Watercress: Members of the mustard family, arugula and watercress are both pungent plants that add spicy taste to salads.

Mesclun: The name refers to a mixture of salad greens that includes both stronger flavored greens, such as arugula, and subtle greens, such as baby spinach. The term comes from the Provençal word for "mixture" and the European practice of gathering a variety of young field greens, herbs, and edible flowers and mixing them in a salad. Packages of mesclun or mixed greens are available in the produce section of most supermarkets.

Vegetables

Many vegetables may be used in salad making, such as the usual tomatoes, peppers, onions, broccoli, asparagus, carrots, and green beans. But there are a number of other vegetables that add a new dimension to salads and are readily available in supermarkets. These include jicama, portobello mushrooms, and avocados, to name a few. Some vegetables are even sold in convenient, ready-to-use packages. You can shorten preparation time by purchasing chopped onions, sliced mushrooms, and shredded carrots and cabbage. I've included tips with some recipes to help you purchase and prepare some of the lesser-known vegetables.

Be sure to visit produce stands, as well as seasonal farmers' markets, for a good selection of the freshest fruits and vegetables. The quality of these ingredients is especially important in salads. While most vegetables are available year round, many—such as tomatoes—have the best flavor when they are in season.

Peeling a Tomato

Whenever a recipe calls for a peeled tomato, first cut an "X" at the tomato's base. Plunge it into boiling water for 30 seconds, then remove with a slotted spoon and plunge immediately into a bowl of ice water. Let the tomato cool for 1 minute. The skin can then be easily removed with a paring knife.

Basic Salad Dressings

Dressing is, quite simply, a sauce for a salad. Its role is to complement, rather than mask, the flavors of the ingredients. It should be light in flavor, well seasoned, and barely coat the greens. Salad dressings are either a mixture of oil and vinegar, called vinaigrette, or a creamy dressing made with mayonnaise or a dairy product.

Vinaigrettes

Simple vinaigrettes are a blend of oil and vinegar seasoned with salt and pepper. Because oil and vinegar do not mix—the oil rises to the top and the vinegar sinks to the bottom—the trickiest part is making sure these two ingredients blend together. There are three ways to prepare vinaigrettes: whisking in a bowl, shaking in a jar with a lid, or processing in a blender or food processor. Whatever method is used, first combine the vinegar and seasonings, then slowly add the oil until the mixture thickens. If prepared in advance, always whisk the vinaigrette just before adding it to the salad. Always dress salads just prior to serving them.

Vinaigrette Recipe

There is no simpler dressing for greens than basic oil and vinegar. The proportions are usually about three parts oil to one part vinegar. Lemon juice can also be used in place of vinegar. Add a pinch of salt and freshly ground pepper, and fresh herbs if desired, and the vinaigrette is done.

Refrigerate vinaigrettes, tightly covered, for about two weeks. Always whisk them just before using.

Oils

While there are many types of oils that can be used to make vinaigrettes, extra-virgin olive oil is by far the most popular. From light, neutral-flavored oils, such as canola, corn, cottonseed, peanut, sunflower, or safflower, to stronger-flavored oils, such as olive, sesame, walnut, almond, and hazelnut, there are many options to try. Remember to store all oils in a cool, dark place and use within one year of purchase.

Olive Oil

Three basic grades of olive oil are available in the supermarket: extra virgin, virgin, and pure. Extra-virgin olive oil is most commonly used for making vinaigrettes. Virgin olive oil is less common, but can also be used for vinaigrettes. Pure olive oil, more commonly labeled as "olive oil," is less delicate in flavor and generally used only for cooking.

The process of making olive oil determines the grade. The first step in extracting the oil is crushing the olives between two stone wheels. Since no heat, steam, or chemicals are used, the oil is called "cold pressed." It is also referred to as "virgin" oil. Depending on the percentage of acidity in the oil, it can also be referred to as "extra-virgin," "superfine virgin," or "fine virgin." Any of these types of cold-pressed oils are the highest quality and have the best flavor. Because they have a low smoke point and burn easily, they are less suitable for use in cooking.

After the first pressing, heat or chemicals are used to assist in further extraction of oil from the olives. Once the oil is refined to remove any elements used in the extraction process, it is designated as "pure." Because pure olive oil has a less delicate flavor and higher acidity, it has a higher smoke point and is best used for cooking, particularly deep-frying.

Experiment and taste different olive oils. Keep several kinds on hand for various uses. French extra-virgin oils, made with ripe black olives, have a sweet, buttery taste and golden hue. Italian extra-virgin oils, made from a blend of black and green olives, are fruitier with a green hue. Oils from Spain and Greece are generally less delicate and used for cooking. California also produces olive oils that are mild and light.

Flavored olive oils are made by adding ingredients, such as garlic, basil, rosemary, and citrus zest, as the olives are being processed. The oil can also be infused with flavor after pressing—a popular activity in home kitchens. But be aware that homemade flavored oils may promote bacterial growth that can cause illness if the oil is not used immediately.

5 Things to Remember about Olive Oil

1. Extra-virgin olive oil is most commonly used for making vinaigrettes.

2. "Light" or "lite" on an olive oil label refers to the flavor of the oil, not the number of calories. All olive oils have 120 calories per tablespoon.

3. Olive oil does not improve with age. If the bottle is dated, do not purchase if it's older than one-and-a-half years. Be sure to use olive oil within one year of opening.

4. Store olive oil in a cool, dark place.

5. Various herbs, spices, and citrus are used to infuse olive oil with flavor. Homemade flavored oils may promote bacterial growth and cause illness if the oil is not used immediately.

Other Oils

Vegetable oils, such as canola, corn, cottonseed, peanut, sunflower, or safflower, are highly refined and very mild in flavor. They are best suited for vinaigrettes where the main flavor comes from other ingredients.

Nut oils, such as sesame, walnut, and hazelnut, have strong flavors and should be used sparingly and blended with milder oil. Sesame oil is available in two varieties—mild, light oil and the more common dark, flavorful Asian type. It's usually complemented by lemon or lime juice and paired with rice wine vinegar. The best walnut and hazelnut oils are imported from France. They blend well with sherry and champagne vinegars. Once opened, they are highly perishable and best stored in the refrigerator.

Vinegars

Vinegar is the natural complement to oil in vinaigrettes. Literally meaning "sour wine," vinegar results when yeast causes wine—or some other alcoholic liquid such as apple cider or Japanese rice wine—to ferment for a second time, turning it acidic. Light and sweet white wine vinegar is made from any variety of white wine. Balsamic vinegar, a specialty of Modena, Italy, is highly aromatic and made from reduced grape juice aged for many years in wood barrels. Although it's highly acidic, it has a wonderfully sweet aftertaste. Red wine vinegar, like the wine from which it is made, is the most robust of the vinegars.

Other Ingredients

In addition to using different oils and vinegars, there are countless ways to create delicious vinaigrettes.

Herbs: Add finely chopped, hearty fresh herbs, such as rosemary, oregano, or thyme and allow the vinaigrette to sit for several hours for the flavors to infuse. Basil, chives, dill, or parsley can be added just before using.

Mustard: Dijon vinaigrette, a classic from France, is made by adding Dijon mustard to the oil and vinegar.

Citrus juices: Fresh lemon, lime, orange, or even grapefruit juice can be used in place of the vinegar in vinaigrettes. Because citrus juice is less acidic than vinegar, the proportion of oil to juice is closer to two parts oil to one part juice.

Sweeteners: A touch of honey, maple syrup, or molasses sweetens vinaigrette and balances the flavors of some salads.

Wines and spirits: A splash of a good-quality wine or spirit, such as port or brandy, adds depth of flavor.

Other ingredients: Chopped pickles, anchovies, capers, horseradish, olives, pickle relish, and garlic can also be added to vinaigrettes in small amounts.

Creamy Dressings

Creamy dressings are better suited to some salads and are a nice alternative to vinaigrettes. These dressings get their thick consistency from the addition of buttermilk, cream, mayonnaise, sour cream, or yogurt. The key to making a good creamy dressing is finding the balance between the acid—vinegar or citrus juice—and the creamy base.

Classic Ranch Dressing

The original version of this popular dressing was created at the Hidden Valley Guest Ranch in Santa Barbara in the 1950s. The term "ranch" has become a generic name not just for the dressing, but also for the buttermilk flavor. If you prefer a thicker dressing, stir in $1/3$ to $1/2$ cup mayonnaise.

1 **clove garlic, peeled**
$1/8$ **teaspoon salt**
$3/4$ **cup buttermilk**
2 **teaspoons fresh lime juice**
1 **tablespoon snipped fresh chives**
1 **tablespoon minced fresh cilantro or parsley**
Salt and ground pepper to taste

Crush the garlic with a fork in a small bowl. Add the salt; stir to make a paste. Add the remaining ingredients; whisk until blended. Refrigerate until serving.

Makes ¾ cup dressing

Poultry

CHICKEN

TURKEY

Asian Chicken Salad

*A creamy peanut butter, sesame, and soy dressing
complements chicken, asparagus, and cabbage in this tasty salad.*

4 boneless, skinless chicken breast halves (4 to 6 ounces each)

1 tablespoon olive oil

Salt and black pepper to taste

1 pound asparagus, ends removed, cut diagonally into thirds

2 red peppers, cored and cut into $^{1}/_{8}$-inch strips

3 cups shredded green cabbage

$^{1}/_{3}$ cup extra-virgin olive oil

2 tablespoons soy sauce

2 tablespoons creamy peanut butter

$1^{1}/_{2}$ tablespoons sesame oil

1 teaspoon minced fresh garlic

1 teaspoon minced fresh ginger root

$^{1}/_{2}$ teaspoon salt

$^{1}/_{4}$ teaspoon pepper

4 green onions, minced

3 tablespoons chopped dry roasted peanuts

1 tablespoon sesame seeds, toasted

3 Asian pears or any crisp fruit such as Granny Smith apples, peeled, cored, and sliced, as a garnish

Preheat the oven to 350°F. Brush both sides of the chicken with 1 tablespoon oil and place in a 13x9x2-inch baking dish. Sprinkle with salt and pepper. Bake for 35 to 40 minutes or until the chicken is no longer pink in the center. Cool; shred the chicken into bite-size pieces with a fork or your fingers.

Meanwhile, cook the asparagus in a large pot of boiling water for 2 to 3 minutes or until crisp-tender. Drain and rinse under cold water. Combine the chicken, asparagus, peppers, and cabbage in a large bowl.

Whisk the extra-virgin olive oil, soy sauce, peanut butter, sesame oil, garlic, ginger root, salt, and pepper in a small bowl. Pour over the chicken mixture; toss to coat. Add the green onions, peanuts and sesame seeds; toss to combine. Serve chilled or at room temperature. Garnish with fruit slices.

Makes 4 servings

TIPS

To toast sesame seeds, cook them in a dry, nonstick skillet over medium heat, stirring constantly, until brown.

Buy firm, straight, uniformly sized asparagus spears with closed, compact tips. The stalks should be crisp, not wilted. Asparagus may be stored for a few days in the refrigerator. Trim ends from bundled stalks. Place asparagus upright in a large glass in an inch of water or before refrigerating wrap the cut ends in a moist paper towel covered with plastic wrap.

NOTE

Asian pears, also called Chinese or apple pears, have a light, sweet taste and a crunchy, very juicy texture. Though not widely available, some varieties are grown in California. If you see them in your produce section, give them a try.

Honey Whole Wheat Dinner Rolls

1 (¹/₄-ounce) package active
   dry yeast

1 cup warm milk (110°F
   to 115°F)

6 tablespoons honey

4 tablespoons melted butter

2 cups whole wheat flour

¹/₂ teaspoon salt

¹/₄ teaspoon baking soda

1¹/₂ to 2 cups all-purpose flour

Dissolve the yeast in the warm milk in a large bowl. Whisk the honey and 3 tablespoons melted butter in a small bowl; stir into the milk mixture. Add the whole wheat flour, salt, and baking soda; stir until combined. Add 1 cup all-purpose flour; knead in the bowl with your hands until the flour is incorporated. Knead in enough of the remaining all-purpose flour, ¹/₂ cup at a time, to form a soft dough. Turn the dough onto a lightly floured surface; knead for 5 minutes or until the dough is smooth and elastic. Shape the dough into a ball and place in a large greased bowl, turning once to grease the entire surface. Cover; let rise in a warm place for 1 hour or until doubled in size. Punch dough down.

Grease two 15x10x1-inch baking sheets. Turn the dough out onto a lightly floured surface; knead 5 to 6 times. Divide the dough into 18 equal pieces; shape each piece into a ball. Place 2 inches apart on the prepared baking sheets. Cover; let rise in a warm place for 20 minutes or until doubled in size.

Preheat the oven to 400°F. Brush the rolls with the remaining 1 tablespoon butter. Bake for 12 to 14 minutes or until lightly browned. Cool on a wire rack. Serve warm or at room temperature. Store in a covered container.

Makes 18 rolls

Chicken Rice Salad

Curried rice, peas, and pineapple lend exotic flavors to this delightful chicken salad.

4 boneless, skinless chicken breast halves (4 to 6 ounces each)

$^1/_4$ cup minced green onions

1 teaspoon minced garlic

1 tablespoon peanut oil

1 $^1/_2$ cups uncooked long-grain rice

3 $^1/_3$ cups chicken broth

2 teaspoons curry powder

$^1/_2$ teaspoon salt

$^1/_2$ cup diced green pepper

1 cup frozen green peas, thawed

1 cup canned pineapple chunks, drained

$^1/_2$ cup pine nuts, toasted

$^3/_4$ cup mango chutney

$^1/_4$ cup chopped fresh mint

2 tablespoons cider vinegar

1 tablespoon peanut oil

1 teaspoon honey mustard

1 teaspoon salt

$^1/_2$ teaspoon pepper

Place the chicken in a large skillet with just enough water to cover; bring to a boil. Reduce heat to medium-low; cover and cook for 10 to 15 minutes or until the chicken is no longer pink in the center. Remove from the pan; cool. Shred the chicken into bite-size pieces with a fork or your fingers.

Meanwhile, cook the green onions and garlic in 1 tablespoon oil in a saucepan over medium heat for 1 minute. Add the rice, broth, curry powder, and salt; bring to a boil. Reduce heat to low and simmer, covered, for 15 minutes or until all of the liquid is absorbed and the rice is tender. Transfer to a large serving bowl; cool.

Add the chicken, green pepper, peas, pineapple, and pine nuts to the rice. Whisk the chutney, mint, cider vinegar, 1 tablespoon oil, honey mustard, salt, and pepper in a small bowl. Pour the dressing over the salad; mix well. Refrigerate for at least 2 hours before serving.

Makes 8 servings

TIPS

Peanut oil, an all-purpose oil derived from peanuts, is pale gold and subtly flavored. It can be heated to high temperatures without smoking, which makes it suitable for deep-frying and sautéing. Substitute vegetable oil if you do not have peanut oil.

To toast the pine nuts, cook them in a dry, nonstick skillet over medium heat, stirring constantly, until brown.

Whole Wheat Rolls

Purchase whole wheat rolls to warm in the oven or serve another easy-to-prepare bread. Or, make the Honey Whole Wheat Dinner Rolls on page 3.

Pineapple-Coconut Bars

Crust

$1/2$ cup (1 stick) butter, softened

$1/4$ cup sugar

$1 1/4$ cups flour, sifted

Filling

1 (20-ounce) can crushed pineapple, well drained

$1/2$ cup sugar

1 egg

1 tablespoon butter, melted

$1 1/2$ cups flaked coconut

Preheat the oven to 350°F. Spray an 8x8x2-inch baking pan with cooking spray.

To make the crust: Beat the butter and sugar in a large bowl with an electric mixer at high speed until well blended. Add the flour; beat at low speed until crumbly. Press evenly onto the bottom and $1/2$ inch up the sides of the prepared pan. Bake for 20 minutes or until lightly browned.

To make the filling: Spread the pineapple evenly over the hot crust. Beat the sugar and egg in a large bowl with an electric mixer at high speed until well blended. Fold in the butter and coconut. Spread evenly over the pineapple. Bake for 25 to 30 minutes or until the coconut is lightly browned. Cool completely on a wire rack. Cut into 16 squares.

Makes 16 bars

Chicken with Lentils and Vegetables

A garden of vegetables—cauliflower, peas, tomatoes, and cucumber—accompany chicken and lentils in this salad.

2 cups chicken broth

1 cup dried lentils

1 cup cauliflower florets

1/3 cup flour

2 teaspoons curry powder

3 boneless, skinless chicken breast halves (4 to 6 ounces each)

3 tablespoons olive oil

1 cup frozen peas, thawed

2 medium tomatoes, seeded and diced

1 cucumber, peeled, seeded, and diced

2 green onions, minced

1 teaspoon salt

1/2 teaspoon pepper

1/4 cup fresh lemon juice

1 teaspoon curry powder

1/4 cup sour cream

2 tablespoons chopped fresh mint

2 small heads Boston lettuce

Bring broth and lentils to a boil in a medium saucepan. Reduce heat to medium-low; cover and simmer for 20 minutes or until lentils are tender. Drain; cool.

Meanwhile, place the cauliflower in a steamer basket. Place the basket in a saucepan over 1 inch of water; bring to a boil. Cover and steam for 5 to 8 minutes or until crisp-tender; drain and rinse with cold water.

Mix flour and 2 teaspoons curry powder in a shallow bowl. Flatten chicken to 1/4 -inch thickness; dredge in the flour mixture. Cook the chicken in oil in a large skillet over medium-high heat for 4 to 5 minutes a side or until the chicken is no longer pink in the center. Cool; cut the chicken into small chunks.

Combine the lentils, cauliflower, peas, tomatoes, cucumber, green onions, salt, and pepper in a large bowl. Add the lemon juice; toss to coat. Add the chicken to the vegetables. Mix 1 teaspoon curry powder, sour cream, and mint in a small bowl. Pour the dressing over the chicken and vegetable mixture; toss to coat. Divide the lettuce among 6 dinner plates; top with salad.

Makes 6 servings

Pita with Hummus

1 (15-ounce) can chick peas
   or garbanzo beans, drained

1 garlic clove, chopped

2 tablespoons fresh lemon juice

2 tablespoons tahini

$^1/_4$ teaspoon ground cumin

$^1/_8$ teaspoon salt

$^1/_8$ teaspoon pepper

2 tablespoons extra-virgin
   olive oil

   Pita chips or pita bread rounds

Process the chick peas and garlic in a food processor until smooth. Combine the lemon juice, tahini, cumin, salt, and pepper in a small bowl. Add to the chickpeas; process until smooth. With the processor on, pour the oil through the food chute; process until combined. Store in the refrigerator until ready to use. Serve with pita chips or warm pita bread rounds.

Makes $^1/_2$ cup

TIPS

To warm pita bread, cut rounds into segments. Place on a baking sheet and broil for 4 to 5 minutes, turning once, until brown.

Prepared hummus—in many different flavors—can be found in the refrigerated section of your local supermarket.

NOTE

Tahini is a smooth, rich paste ground from sesame seeds. It is used in Middle Eastern cooking to enrich the flavor and texture of dishes. Jars and cans of tahini are found in Middle Eastern markets and in the international section of your local supermarket.

Peaches with Yogurt

6 fresh peaches, peeled, pitted
   and cut into $^1/_2$-inch slices

1$^1/_2$ cups vanilla yogurt

3 teaspoons honey

Place peach slices into individual dessert bowls. Whisk the yogurt and honey in a small bowl; pour over the peaches.

Makes 6 servings

Easy Cobb Salad

This classic salad comes together in a snap using convenience ingredients from the supermarket.

1 large head iceberg lettuce, chopped

4 hard-cooked eggs, peeled and diced

2 avocados, peeled, pitted, and diced

4 cups cooked, chopped chicken

2 tomatoes, chopped

4 tablespoons bacon bits

4 tablespoons crumbled blue cheese

$^1\!/\!_4$ cup red wine vinegar

$^1\!/\!_2$ teaspoon Worcestershire sauce

$^1\!/\!_2$ teaspoon Dijon mustard

$^1\!/\!_3$ cup extra-virgin olive oil

Divide the lettuce among 4 dinner plates. Arrange the eggs, avocados, chicken, tomatoes, bacon bits, and blue cheese on top of the lettuce. (*For a nice presentation, assemble the ingredients in rows in the order listed.*)

Whisk the vinegar, Worcestershire sauce, and mustard in a small bowl. Add the oil; whisk until combined. Pour the dressing over the salad.

Makes 4 servings

TIPS

Use leftover chicken or purchase cooked chicken at the supermarket.

Select avocados that yield to gentle pressure and store them in the refrigerator. If an avocado is firm, ripen at room temperature for several days or, more quickly, in a closed paper bag.

To pit an avocado, do not remove the skin. Cut the avocado in half down to the pit. Twist the halves to separate. Holding the half with the pit in one hand, carefully strike the pit with the blade of a sturdy knife to wedge the blade firmly into the pit. Twist and lift the knife to remove the pit.

To scoop out and slice or dice an avocado, slide a large spoon between the avocado flesh and the skin. Scoop out the flesh in one piece. Place it, cut side down, on a work surface. Slice with a small knife. Cut across the slices to dice the avocado to the desired size.

Breadsticks

Pop refrigerated breadsticks or biscuits into the oven for a quick accompaniment to this salad.

Lemon Bars

Crust

  1 **cup flour**

  ¹/₄ **cup confectioners' sugar**

  ¹/₂ **cup (1 stick) butter, softened**

Filling

  2 **eggs**

  1 **cup sugar**

  2 **tablespoons flour**

  2 **tablespoons fresh lemon juice**

Frosting

1 ¹/₂ **cups confectioners' sugar, sifted**

  2 **tablespoons butter, softened**

  1 **tablespoon milk**

  1 **teaspoon vanilla extract**

Preheat the oven to 350°F.

To make the crust: Blend the flour and confectioners' sugar in a large bowl. Add the butter. Beat with an electric mixer at high speed until combined. Press onto the bottom and ¹/₂ inch up the sides of an 8x8x2-inch baking pan. Bake for 20 minutes or until lightly browned; set aside.

To make the filling: Beat the eggs in a large bowl with an electric mixer at high speed until frothy. Add the sugar, flour, and lemon juice. Beat at low speed just until combined. Spread evenly over the warm crust. Bake for 20 minutes or until set. Cool on a wire rack for at least 30 minutes.

To make the frosting: Beat the confectioners' sugar, butter, milk, and vanilla in a large bowl with an electric mixer at medium speed until smooth. Spread evenly over the cooled bars. Refrigerate for at least 1 hour before serving. Cut into 16 squares.

Makes 16 bars

Creamy Chicken Salad

Fresh dill adds a wonderful flavor to this classic chicken salad recipe.

4 boneless, skinless chicken breast halves (4 to 6 ounces each)

³/4 cup diced celery

2 green onions, minced

¹/2 cup mayonnaise

2 teaspoons chopped fresh dill or 2 teaspoons dried dill weed

¹/2 teaspoon salt

¹/4 teaspoon pepper

Fresh pineapple, peeled, cored, and cut into rings, or canned pineapple rings (optional)

Place the chicken in a large skillet with just enough water to cover; bring to a boil. Reduce heat to medium-low; cover and cook for 10 to 15 minutes or until the chicken is no longer pink in the center. Remove from the pan; cool. Shred the chicken into bite-size pieces with a fork or your fingers.

Combine the chicken, celery, and green onions in a large bowl. Whisk the mayonnaise, dill, salt, and pepper in a small bowl. Add the mayonnaise mixture to the chicken; mix well. Refrigerate at least 4 hours before serving. Serve over pineapple rings, if desired.

Makes 4 servings

TIPS

For a more dramatic presentation, cut 2 fresh pineapples in half lengthwise and scoop out the fruit. Serve the salad in the pineapples; save the fruit and serve it mixed with other fresh fruit for dessert.

Choose a fresh-looking pineapple that seems heavy for its size. It should have a sweet, tropical fragrance and deep green leaves.

NOTE

Pineapples are available year-round, but March to July is their peak season. Most of those sold in U.S. markets come from Hawaii, Puerto Rico, Costa Rica, and Mexico. Since pineapples are harvested when fully ripe, they are shipped by air and reach most major markets within thirty-six hours after harvesting.

Blueberry Streusel Muffins

Streusel

- 2 **tablespoons brown sugar**
- ¹/₄ **teaspoon cinnamon**
- 2 **tablespoons butter, cold and cut into small pieces**
- ¹/₂ **cup chopped walnuts**

Muffins

- 2 **cups flour**
- 2 **teaspoons baking powder**
- ¹/₄ **teaspoon salt**
- ²/₃ **cup sugar**
- 6 **tablespoons butter, softened**
- 1 **teaspoon vanilla extract**
- 2 **eggs**
- ¹/₂ **cup milk**
- 2 **cups fresh blueberries**

Preheat oven to 375°F. Line muffin cups with foil liners or spray unlined cups with cooking spray.

To make the streusel: Combine the brown sugar and cinnamon in a small bowl; cut in the butter with a pastry blender or 2 knives until the mixture resembles coarse crumbs. Stir in the nuts; set aside.

To make the muffins: Sift together the flour, baking powder, and salt; set aside. Beat the sugar, butter, and vanilla in a large bowl with an electric mixer at high speed until well blended. Add the eggs one at a time, beating well after each addition. Add the flour mixture alternately with the milk, beating at low speed after each addition. Add the blueberries; stir gently with a spatula until combined. Spoon the batter into muffin cups. Sprinkle streusel over the batter. Bake for 25 to 30 minutes or until muffins and topping are lightly browned. Cool completely in the pan on a wire rack.

Makes 12 muffins

Fresh Fruit with Yogurt

Mix blueberries, strawberries, grapes, nectarine slices, and pineapple chunks with peach yogurt for a simple and tasty dessert.

Curried Chicken Salad

Raisins and cashews add the crunch and curry adds the flavor to this delicious salad.

4 **boneless, skinless chicken breast halves (4 to 6 ounces each)**

1 **tablespoon olive oil**

Salt and pepper to taste

1 1/2 **cups diced celery**

1 **cup golden raisins**

1 **cup roasted salted cashews**

1 1/2 **cups mayonnaise**

2 **tablespoons curry powder**

2 **teaspoons ground coriander**

1 **tablespoon white wine vinegar**

1 **tablespoon fresh lemon juice**

1 **tablespoon honey**

1 **teaspoon salt**

1/2 **teaspoon pepper**

Preheat the oven to 350°F. Coat the chicken with oil and place in a 13x9x2-inch baking dish. Sprinkle with salt and pepper. Bake for 35 to 40 minutes or until the chicken is no longer pink in the center. Cool; shred the chicken into bite-size pieces with a fork or your fingers. Place the chicken in a large bowl; add the celery, raisins, and cashews.

Whisk the mayonnaise, curry powder, coriander, vinegar, lemon juice, honey, salt, and pepper in a small bowl. Add the mayonnaise mixture to the chicken; mix well. Refrigerate at least 4 hours before serving.

Makes 6 servings

TIP

Don't worry about having leftover salad—the flavors are even better the next day!

Whole Wheat Rolls

Purchase whole wheat rolls to warm in the oven or serve another easy-to-prepare bread. Or, make the Honey Whole Wheat Dinner Rolls on page 3.

Apple Crumble Cake

Cake

2 1/4 **cups flour**

2 **teaspoons baking soda**

1/2 **teaspoon ground nutmeg**

1/2 **teaspoon cinnamon**

1/4 **teaspoon salt**

1/4 **teaspoon ground cloves**

1 **cup granulated sugar**

1/2 **cup packed light brown sugar**

1/2 **cup shortening**

1 **cup buttermilk**

2 **eggs, beaten**

4 **medium Golden Delicious apples, peeled, cored, and cut into** 1/4-**inch slices**

Topping

1/2 **cup coarsely chopped pecans**

1/4 **cup granulated sugar**

1/4 **cup packed light brown sugar**

1/8 **teaspoon cinnamon**

Preheat the oven to 350°F. Grease and flour a 13x9x2-inch baking pan.

To make the cake: Sift together the flour, baking soda, nutmeg, cinnamon, salt, and cloves; set aside. Beat the sugars and shortening in a large bowl with an electric mixer at high speed until blended. Add the buttermilk and eggs; beat until smooth. Add the flour mixture; beat until well combined. Fold in the apples. Pour into the prepared pan, spreading evenly.

To make the topping: Combine the pecans, sugars, and cinnamon in a small bowl. Sprinkle over the batter. Bake for 45 to 50 minutes or until a wooden pick inserted into the center comes out clean. Cool on a wire rack.

Makes 15 servings

TIP

This fresh apple cake is so good that you'll serve it for breakfast, too!

Crisp Chicken Salad

Buttermilk is the perfect dressing for crispy fried chicken strips on top of crunchy lettuce and vegetables.

³/₄ **cup buttermilk**

¹/₄ **cup mayonnaise**

  2 **tablespoons sour cream**

  2 **tablespoons fresh lemon juice**

¹/₄ **teaspoon salt**

¹/₈ **teaspoon white pepper**

¹/₈ **teaspoon garlic powder**

¹/₂ **cup bread crumbs**

¹/₂ **cup cornmeal**

  1 **tablespoon paprika**

  1 **teaspoon chili powder**

  1 **teaspoon ground cumin**

¹/₂ **tablespoon onion powder**

¹/₂ **teaspoon salt**

¹/₂ **teaspoon black pepper**

  4 **boneless, skinless chicken breast halves (4 to 6 ounces each), cut into strips**

  1 **medium head iceberg lettuce, chopped**

  1 **cup shredded carrots**

  2 **tomatoes, sliced**

  1 **small onion, sliced**

  1 **small green pepper, sliced**

Whisk the buttermilk, mayonnaise, sour cream, lemon juice, salt, white pepper, and garlic powder in a small bowl; refrigerate.

Preheat oven to 400°F. Spray a 13x9x2-inch baking dish with cooking spray.

Combine the bread crumbs, cornmeal, paprika, chili powder, cumin, onion powder, salt, and black pepper in a resealable plastic bag. Add the chicken; toss to coat. Place chicken in the prepared baking dish; bake for 18 to 20 minutes or until the chicken is no longer pink in the center.

Divide the lettuce among 4 dinner plates; top with carrots, tomatoes, onion, green pepper, and chicken strips. Drizzle with dressing.

Makes 4 servings

TIPS

To save time, purchase shredded carrots in a bag in the produce section of your local supermarket.

For another timesaver, purchase pre-cut raw chicken tenders in the refrigerated meat section of your local supermarket.

Buttermilk Biscuits

Pop refrigerated biscuits into the oven for a quick accompaniment to this salad. Have more time? Bake biscuits from scratch. See page 35.

Apple Crisp

Topping

- ¹/₄ **cup packed brown sugar**
- ¹/₄ **cup old-fashioned rolled oats**
- 2 **tablespoons flour**
- ¹/₂ **teaspoon cinnamon**
- 3 **tablespoons butter, cold and cut into small pieces**
- ¹/₄ **cup pecans, chopped and lightly toasted**

Filling

- 3 **tablespoons sugar**
- 2 **teaspoons flour**
- 4 **medium Golden Delicious apples, peeled, cored, and cut into ¹/₂-inch slices**

Preheat the oven to 350°F. Spray four 8-ounce ramekins with cooking spray.

To make the topping: Combine the brown sugar, oats, flour, and cinnamon in a small bowl. Cut in the butter with a pastry blender or 2 knives until the mixture resembles coarse crumbs. Stir in the nuts; set aside.

To make the filling: Combine the sugar and flour in a resealable plastic bag. Add the apples; toss to coat. Spoon the mixture into the prepared ramekins. Sprinkle the topping evenly over the fruit, lightly pressing it in place. Bake for 20 to 25 minutes, until the filling is bubbling. Serve warm or at room temperature.

Makes 4 servings

TIPS

To toast the pecans, place them on a baking sheet and toast in a 375°F oven for 10 to 12 minutes or until lightly brown.

Assemble all of the ingredients in the ramekins before dinner and bake the crisp while you eat.

Grilled Chicken & Green Bean Salad with Blueberry Relish

Fresh summer blueberries are an integral part of this tasty meal.

1 pound green beans, washed and trimmed

2 tablespoons white wine vinegar

1 tablespoon honey mustard

4 tablespoons extra-virgin olive oil

1 ½ cups fresh blueberries

1 tablespoon sugar

2 tablespoons chopped red onion

1 teaspoon balsamic vinegar

3 teaspoons fresh lemon juice

4 boneless, skinless chicken breast halves (6 to 8 ounces each)

¼ teaspoon salt

¼ teaspoon pepper

4 cups torn romaine lettuce

Place the green beans in a steamer basket. Place the basket in a saucepan over 1 inch of water; bring to a boil. Cover and steam for 5 minutes or until crisp-tender; drain and set aside to cool.

Whisk the white wine vinegar, mustard, and oil in a small bowl; set aside.

Process the blueberries, sugar, red onion, balsamic vinegar, and lemon juice in a food processor until coarsely chopped; set aside.

Season the chicken with salt and pepper. Prepare a medium-hot fire in a charcoal or gas grill; oil the grill grate with cooking spray. Grill the chicken for 6 to 8 minutes a side over medium-high heat until the chicken is firm and no longer pink in the center; cut into thin slices.

Toss the lettuce and green beans with the dressing. Divide the lettuce mixture among 4 dinner plates; top with chicken slices and blueberry relish.

Makes 4 servings

NOTE

Michigan and Indiana harvest 40% of all the cultivated blueberries in America. New Jersey, Florida, Georgia, Louisiana, Mississippi, North Carolina, Oregon, and Washington grow the remainder. The North American harvest runs from mid-April through early October with the peak harvest in July. In the winter, fresh blueberries are imported from South America, Australia, and New Zealand.

Blueberry Biscuits

2 cups flour

¼ cup sugar

2 teaspoons baking powder

½ teaspoon baking soda

¼ teaspoon salt

¼ cup butter, cold and cut into pieces

1 egg

1 (6-ounce) container plain yogurt

1 teaspoon grated lemon zest

3 teaspoons fresh lemon juice

1 cup fresh blueberries

Preheat the oven to 400°F. Spray two 15x10x1-inch baking sheets with cooking spray. Whisk the flour, sugar, baking powder, soda, and salt in a medium bowl. Cut in the butter with a pastry blender or 2 knives until the mixture resembles coarse crumbs. Beat the egg in a small bowl; mix in the yogurt and lemon zest. Stir into the flour mixture just until moistened; fold in blueberries. Drop the dough by rounded tablespoons 2 inches apart onto prepared baking sheets. Bake for 15 to 18 minutes or until lightly browned. Cool on a wire rack for 15 minutes. Serve warm.

Makes 12 biscuits

Blueberries in Irish Cream

2 cups fresh blueberries

1 (6-ounce) container vanilla yogurt

¼ cup Irish cream liqueur

Divide the blueberries among 4 dessert dishes. Combine the yogurt and liqueur in a small bowl. Spoon over the berries in each dish. Serve immediately or refrigerate, covered, for up to 8 hours.

Makes 4 servings

Grilled Chicken Pesto Salad

Grilled chicken flavored with pesto, bruschetta, and fresh blueberries in cream make this a delicious summer meal!

3 boneless, skinless chicken breast halves (6 to 8 ounces each)

Salt and pepper to taste

5 cups chopped romaine lettuce

1 cup diced zucchini

2 cups chopped fresh tomato

1 tablespoon extra-virgin olive oil

4 tablespoons Pesto (recipe below)

1 1/2 cups shredded fresh Parmesan cheese

Season chicken with salt and pepper. Prepare a medium-hot fire in a charcoal or gas grill; oil the grill grate with cooking spray. Grill the chicken for 6 to 8 minutes a side over medium-high heat until the chicken is firm and no longer pink in the center; cut into bite size pieces.

In a large bowl, toss the lettuce, zucchini, and tomato with the oil. Add 3 tablespoons pesto, 1 tablespoon at a time; toss well. Add the chicken and remaining 1 tablespoon pesto; toss to coat. Add salt and pepper to taste. Sprinkle with the Parmesan cheese; toss to combine.

Makes 4 servings

Pesto

2 tablespoons pine nuts, toasted

2 teaspoons coarsely chopped garlic

3 cups loosely packed fresh basil leaves

2 tablespoons grated fresh Parmesan cheese

3 teaspoons fresh lemon juice

1/8 teaspoon salt

1/8 teaspoon pepper

4 tablespoons extra-virgin olive oil

Process the pine nuts and garlic in a food processor until ground. Add the basil, cheese, lemon juice, salt, and pepper; process until smooth. With the processor on, slowly pour the oil through the food chute; process until combined. Store in the refrigerator until ready to use.

Makes 1/2 cup

TIPS

To toast pine nuts, cook them in a dry, nonstick skillet over medium heat, stirring constantly, until brown.

Make a large batch of pesto in the summer when fresh basil leaves are plentiful. Store it in small containers in the freezer to use all winter.

Prepared pesto can be purchased in either the refrigerated or Italian section of your local supermarket.

Bruschetta

8 **large plum tomatoes, seeded and diced**

10 **large fresh basil leaves, cut into thin strips**

3 **tablespoons shredded fresh Parmesan cheese**

3 **tablespoons extra-virgin olive oil**

1/4 **teaspoon salt**

1/8 **teaspoon pepper**

16 **slices Italian bread, cut 1/2- to 3/4-inch thick**

2 **garlic cloves, cut in half**

Combine the tomatoes, basil, cheese, oil, salt, and pepper in a small bowl. Toast the bread until lightly golden on both sides. While still warm, rub one side of the toast with the cut side of the garlic; top with the tomato mixture.

Makes 3 cups tomato mixture

Blueberries in Frangelico Cream

2 **cups fresh blueberries**

1 **(6-ounce) container low-fat vanilla yogurt**

1/4 **cup Frangelico liqueur**

Divide the blueberries among 4 dessert dishes. Combine the yogurt and liqueur in a small bowl. Spoon over the berries in each dish. Serve immediately or refrigerate, covered, for up to 8 hours.

Makes 4 servings

Grilled Chicken Caesar Salad

Everyone should experience making a Caesar salad from scratch at least once. This version is topped with grilled chicken and served as the main course.

2 cups cubed slightly stale French or Italian bread

2 tablespoons extra-virgin olive oil

1 teaspoon garlic powder

4 boneless, skinless chicken breast halves (4 to 6 ounces each)

Salt and pepper to taste

3 garlic cloves, peeled

¹/₂ teaspoon salt

3 anchovy fillets

2 teaspoons red wine vinegar

1 teaspoon Worcestershire sauce

¹/₄ teaspoon pepper

¹/₃ cup extra-virgin olive oil

1 large head of Romaine lettuce, torn into small pieces

¹/₃ cup shredded fresh Parmesan cheese

Preheat oven to 400°F. Coat a 15x10x1-inch baking sheet with cooking spray.

Arrange the bread cubes on the prepared baking sheet; brush with 2 tablespoons oil and sprinkle with garlic powder. Bake for 5 minutes. Turn cubes over and bake for 5 to 6 minutes or until lightly browned; set aside.

Season the chicken with salt and pepper. Prepare a medium-hot fire in a charcoal or gas grill; oil the grill grate with cooking spray. Grill the chicken for 4 to 6 minutes a side over medium-high heat until the chicken is firm and no longer pink in the center; cut into thin slices.

In the bottom of a large salad bowl, crush the garlic with a fork. Add the salt; stir to make a paste. Add the anchovies; crush them with a fork to combine. Add the vinegar, Worcestershire sauce, and pepper; whisk to combine. Add ¹/₃ cup oil; whisk until thickened. Add the lettuce leaves and croutons to the bowl; toss to coat.

Arrange the lettuce mixture on 4 dinner plates. Top with sliced chicken; sprinkle with cheese.

Makes 4 servings

TIP

To save time, purchase prepared croutons and Caesar salad dressing from your local supermarket.

NOTE

For food safety reasons, we have eliminated the raw egg in the dressing.

Apricot Hazelnut Biscotti

1 cup sugar

1/3 cup butter, softened

2 teaspoons baking powder

1/2 teaspoon ground cardamom

2 eggs

1 teaspoon vanilla extract

2 cups flour

3/4 cup hazelnuts, chopped

3/4 cup chopped dried apricots

Preheat the oven to 375°F. Spray a 15x10x1-inch baking sheet with cooking spray.

Beat the sugar and butter in a large bowl with an electric mixer at high speed until fluffy. Beat in the baking powder and cardamom. Add the eggs and vanilla; beat until well blended. Stir in the flour by hand until completely incorporated. Stir in the hazelnuts and dried apricots. Using flour-coated hands, divide the dough into halves. Shape each half into a 9x3-inch log on the prepared baking sheet. Refrigerate for at least 30 minutes or up to 1 hour.

Bake for 25 to 30 minutes, until a wooden pick inserted into the centers comes out clean. Cool on the pan for 15 minutes. *Reduce the oven temperature to 325°F.*

With a serrated knife, cut each log diagonally into 1/2-inch-thick slices. Place the slices, cut sides down, on the same baking sheet. Bake at 325°F for 8 minutes. Turn the slices over; bake for 8 to 10 minutes, until dry and crisp. Cool completely on a wire rack. Store in an airtight container at room temperature for up to 2 days or freeze for up to 6 months.

Makes 3 dozen cookies

TIP

For an extra-special touch, dip the biscotti halfway into melted semisweet chocolate. Place on waxed paper. Let stand until the chocolate is set. Store layered between sheets of waxed paper.

Grilled Chicken with Mango Salsa

Green cabbage stir-fried in sesame oil makes a nice bed for grilled chicken topped with mango salsa.

2 cups peeled, diced mango

¼ cup minced red pepper

¼ cup chopped fresh cilantro

1 teaspoon finely grated lime zest

4 tablespoons fresh lime juice

4 boneless, skinless chicken breast halves (6 to 8 ounces each)

Salt and pepper to taste

2 teaspoons sesame oil

4 cups thinly sliced green cabbage

2 teaspoons sesame seeds

Combine the mango, pepper, cilantro, lime zest, and lime juice in a bowl; let stand at room temperature for at least 30 minutes.

Season chicken with salt and pepper. Prepare a medium-hot fire in a charcoal or gas grill; oil the grill grate with cooking spray. Grill the chicken for 6 to 8 minutes a side over medium-high heat until the chicken is firm and no longer pink in the center; cut into thin slices.

Heat the oil in a large skillet. Add the cabbage and sesame seeds and sauté for 2 to 3 minutes or until the cabbage is crisp-tender.

Divide the cabbage among 4 dinner plates; top with chicken slices and salsa.

Makes 4 servings

TIP

A fresh mango has a long, flat seed that runs down the center, which makes it tricky to cut. Here's one easy method for cutting a mango into cubes:

1. Cut both ends off the mango to determine the seed location.
2. Hold the mango upright on a cutting board. Cut down about ½ inch to the right of the seed. Repeat on the opposite side of the fruit, forming 2 oval-shaped halves.
3. Score the flesh in a crisscross pattern, cutting up to but not through the skin.
4. Holding 1 mango half with both hands, use your thumbs to press against the skin, popping up the mango cubes. Cut across the bottom of the cubes to separate them from the skin.

Grilled Chicken with Mango Salsa

Breadsticks

Pineapple-Mango Bars

Breadsticks

Pop refrigerated breadsticks or biscuits into the oven for a quick accompaniment to this salad.

Pineapple-Mango Bars

Filling

   2 **cups chopped fresh pineapple**
   2 **cups chopped fresh mango**
 ³/₄ **cup packed brown sugar**
 ¹/₂ **cup fresh orange juice**
   1 **teaspoon grated orange zest**
   1 **teaspoon grated lemon zest**
 ¹/₂ **teaspoon ground allspice**

Crust

   1 **cup (2 sticks) butter, softened**
 ¹/₂ **cup sugar**
   1 **teaspoon coconut extract**
 ¹/₈ **teaspoon salt**
   2 **cups flour**

To make the filling: Combine the pineapple, mango, brown sugar, orange juice, orange zest, lemon zest, and allspice in a heavy, medium saucepan. Bring to a boil over medium heat. Reduce the heat to low; simmer for 1 hour and 30 minutes or until the fruit is tender and the liquid thickens, stirring frequently. Cool slightly.

To make the crust: Beat the butter, sugar, coconut extract, and salt in a large bowl with an electric mixer at high speed until blended. Gradually add the flour, beating at low speed just until a soft dough forms. Divide the dough into 2 pieces, one slightly larger than the other. Shape each dough piece into a square. Wrap in plastic wrap; refrigerate for 1 hour.

Preheat the oven to 375°F. Spray a 9x9x2-inch baking dish with cooking spray.

Roll out the larger dough square to a 10-inch square on a lightly floured surface. Press onto the bottom and ¹/₂ inch up the sides of the prepared dish. Spoon the filling into the crust, spreading evenly. Roll out the remaining dough to a 9-inch square on a lightly floured surface. Cut into nine 1-inch-wide strips. Place 4 strips over the filling, spacing evenly. Place the remaining 5 strips diagonally over the top, forming a lattice. Trim any excess dough even with the edges of the pan.

Bake for 50 minutes or until the crust is lightly browned and the filling is bubbling. Cool completely in the pan on a wire rack. Cut into 16 squares. Can be made the day before.

Makes 16 bars

Melon Chicken Salad

Chicken, juicy melons and cucumbers, crunchy Chinese cabbage, and peanuts are tossed in a honey, soy, peanut dressing for a tasty salad.

3 boneless, skinless chicken breast halves (6 to 8 ounces each)

2 tablespoons soy sauce

1/4 cup rice vinegar

2 tablespoons soy sauce

2 tablespoons peanut butter

1 tablespoon honey

1 teaspoon sesame oil

2 cups honeydew melon strips (2x 1/4-inch)

2 cups cantaloupe strips (2x 1/4-inch)

1 cup peeled and seeded cucumber strips (2x 1/4-inch)

1/4 cup minced green onion

1/2 head napa cabbage, cut cross-wise into thin strips

1/4 cup chopped fresh cilantro

1/4 cup chopped dry roasted peanuts

Place the chicken in a large skillet with 2 tablespoons soy sauce and just enough water to cover; bring to a boil. Reduce heat to medium-low; cover and cook for 12 to 17 minutes or until the chicken is no longer pink in the center. Remove from the pan; cool. Shred the chicken into bite-size pieces with a fork or your fingers.

Whisk the rice vinegar, 2 tablespoons soy sauce, peanut butter, honey, and sesame oil in a large bowl. Add the chicken, melon, cantaloupe, cucumber, and green onion; toss to coat. Stir in the cabbage, cilantro, and peanuts. Serve chilled or at room temperature.

Makes 6 servings

TIP

Selecting ripe cantaloupes or melons can sometimes be tricky. Look for fruit that have a good fragrance, that are firm with a little give (not overly soft), and that are heavy for their size. Shake the melon or cantaloupe. If you hear liquid sloshing around inside, the fruit is probably overripe. Avoid fruit that show cracks, shriveling, or other obvious signs of poor quality. Ripen melons and cantaloupes at room temperature—it can take up to 4 days. Wrap cut melons, with the seeds intact, and refrigerate for up to 3 days.

NOTE

Napa cabbage, otherwise known as Chinese cabbage, has white ribs and veiny green leaves. It's commonly used in Asian cooking and can be found year-round in the produce section of your local supermarket.

Orange-Fig Bars

Crust

1 ³/₄ **cups flour**

1 **teaspoon baking powder**

¹/₄ **teaspoon salt**

6 **tablespoons butter, softened**

¹/₄ **cup sugar**

¹/₄ **cup honey**

1 **teaspoon vanilla extract**

1 **egg**

Filling

2 **cups dried figs, coarsely chopped**

2 **tablespoons sugar**

1 **tablespoon grated orange zest**

¹/₄ **cup boiling water**

3 **tablespoons fresh orange juice**

2 **tablespoons honey**

1 **teaspoon vanilla extract**

1 **egg yolk**

1 **tablespoon milk**

To make the crust: Sift together the flour, baking powder, and salt; set aside. Beat the butter and sugar in a large bowl with an electric mixer at high speed until well blended. Add the honey, vanilla, and egg; beat well. Gradually add the flour mixture, beating at low speed just until a soft dough forms. Divide the dough into halves. Shape each half into a small square. Wrap in plastic wrap; refrigerate for 1 hour.

Preheat the oven to 375°F. Spray a 9x9x2-inch baking dish with cooking spray.

To make the filling: Process the figs, sugar, and orange zest in a food processor until the figs are minced. Combine the boiling water, orange juice, honey, and vanilla in a small bowl until combined. With the processor on, add the juice mixture to the fig mixture, processing until well blended.

Roll out 1 dough half to a 9-inch square on a lightly floured surface. Press onto the bottom of the prepared dish. Spread the fig filling evenly over the dough. Roll out the remaining dough to a 9-inch square on a lightly floured surface. Place over the filling. Combine the egg yolk and milk in a small bowl. Brush over the top crust.

Bake for 30 minutes or until the crust is lightly browned. Cool completely on a wire rack. Cut into 20 squares.

Makes 20 bars

Orange Chicken Spinach Salad

*Baby spinach, mushrooms, and oranges tossed with
an orange vinaigrette pair nicely with grilled chicken.*

2/3 **cup fresh orange juice**

1/4 **cup honey**

2 **teaspoons minced garlic**

2 **teaspoons grated orange zest**

1 **teaspoon dried thyme**

6 **boneless, skinless chicken breast
halves (6 to 8 ounces each)**

Salt and pepper to taste

3 **navel oranges**

1/4 **cup fresh orange juice**

1/4 **cup white wine vinegar**

2 **green onions, minced**

6 **tablespoons extra-virgin
olive oil**

1 **cup sliced mushrooms**

1 **(9-ounce) package baby
spinach**

1/2 **cup sliced almonds**

Combine 2/3 cup orange juice, honey, garlic, orange zest, and
thyme in a resealable plastic bag. Add chicken breasts; turn
to coat. Cover and refrigerate for at least 4 hours, turning
chicken occasionally; discard the marinade.

Season chicken with salt and pepper. Prepare a medium-hot
fire in a charcoal or gas grill; oil the grill grate with cooking
spray. Grill the chicken for 6 to 8 minutes a side over medium-
high heat until the chicken is firm and no longer pink in the
center; cut into thin slices.

Cut off and discard both ends of the oranges. Stand each one
upright on a cutting board. Cut downward in vertical strips
following the curve of the orange to remove the peel and
pith. Working over a bowl to catch the juice, cut down on
either side of each membrane to release and lift out the
individual orange sections; set aside.

Whisk 1/4 cup orange juice, vinegar, and green onions in
a small bowl. Slowly add the oil and whisk to blend.

Combine the orange segments, mushrooms, spinach, and
almonds in a large bowl. Add the dressing; toss
to coat. Divide the salad among 4 dinner plates; top with
chicken slices.

Makes 6 servings

TIP

The outermost, colored part of orange skin is called the zest.
The white part underneath the zest is the pith and has a bitter
taste. For grated zest, use the fine holes on a box-shaped
grater or a rasp grater. Since it's easier to remove zest from
a whole orange, zest it before cutting.

Delicious Salad Meals

Breadsticks

Pop refrigerated breadsticks or biscuits into the oven for a quick accompaniment to this salad.

White Chocolate and Orange Cookies

2 1/4 **cups flour**

1 **teaspoon baking soda**

1/2 **teaspoon salt**

1 **cup (2 sticks) butter, softened**

1/2 **cup granulated sugar**

1/2 **cup packed light brown sugar**

1 **egg**

1 **tablespoon grated orange zest**

1 **teaspoon orange extract**

1 **(12-ounce) package white chocolate chips**

1/2 **cup macadamia nuts, chopped**

1/2 **cup flaked coconut**

Preheat the oven to 350°F. Grease 2 cookie sheets.

Sift together the flour, baking soda, and salt; set aside. Beat the butter and sugars in a large bowl with an electric mixer at high speed until fluffy. Beat in the egg, orange zest, and orange extract. Gradually add the flour mixture, beating at low speed just until combined. Stir in the white chocolate chips, macadamia nuts, and coconut by hand.

Drop the dough by rounded teaspoonfuls 2 inches apart onto the prepared cookie sheets. Bake for about 12 minutes or until lightly browned. Cool on the pans for 10 minutes. Remove to wire racks; cool completely.

Makes 3 dozen cookies

Pistachio Chicken Salad

Pan-fried chicken, coated with bread crumbs and pistachios, makes a tasty meal on top of greens tossed with a tomato vinaigrette dressing.

3/4 cup plain bread crumbs

2 tablespoons ground pistachios

1 teaspoon grated lemon zest

1/2 teaspoon salt

1/2 teaspoon pepper

4 boneless, skinless chicken breast halves (4 to 6 ounces each)

3 tablespoons olive oil

1/4 cup red wine vinegar

2 tablespoons ketchup

2 tablespoons minced fresh basil or 1 teaspoon dried basil

1/2 teaspoon Worcestershire sauce

1/3 cup extra-virgin olive oil

8 cups gourmet salad greens

4 large plum tomatoes, sliced

Combine the bread crumbs, pistachios, lemon zest, salt, and pepper in a shallow bowl. Flatten the chicken to 1/4-inch thickness; dredge in the bread crumb mixture. Cook the chicken in olive oil in a large skillet over medium-high heat for 4 to 5 minutes a side or until the chicken is no longer pink in the center; cut into thin slices.

Whisk the vinegar, ketchup, basil, and Worcestershire sauce in a bowl. Add the extra-virgin olive oil; whisk until combined. Place the salad greens and tomatoes in a large bowl. Pour the dressing over the greens; toss to coat. Arrange the salad on 4 dinner plates; top with the chicken slices.

Makes 4 servings

Pistachio Chicken Salad

Olive Bruschetta

Pear Cake with Pine Nuts

Olive Bruschetta

1 (4.25-ounce) can chopped ripe black olives

1 teaspoon minced garlic

2 tablespoons minced parsley

3 tablespoons extra-virgin olive oil

1 loaf Italian bread, cut into $^1/_2$- to $^3/_4$-inch-thick slices

$^1/_4$ cup shredded fresh Parmesan cheese

Combine the olives, garlic, parsley, and oil in a small bowl. Toast the bread until lightly golden on both sides. Spread a small amount of the olive mixture on each piece of toast; sprinkle with the cheese.

Makes ¾ cup olive spread

Pear Cake with Pine Nuts

$1^1/_4$ cups flour

$^3/_4$ cup sugar

$^1/_8$ teaspoon salt

$^1/_4$ cup ($^1/_2$ stick) butter, cold and cut into small pieces

2 tablespoons pine nuts, toasted

$^1/_4$ teaspoon cinnamon

$^1/_3$ cup sour cream

$^1/_4$ cup milk

1 egg

1 teaspoon vanilla extract

$^1/_2$ teaspoon baking powder

$^1/_4$ teaspoon baking soda

2 Bartlett pears, peeled, cored, and cut into $^1/_4$-inch slices

Preheat the oven to 350°F. Spray a 9-inch round cake pan with cooking spray.

Combine the flour, sugar, and salt in a large bowl. Cut in the butter with a pastry blender or 2 knives until the mixture resembles coarse crumbs. Remove $^1/_3$ cup of the flour mixture to a small bowl; stir in the pine nuts and cinnamon and set aside.

To the remaining flour mixture, add the sour cream, milk, egg, vanilla, baking powder, and baking soda. Beat with an electric mixer at high speed until well blended. Pour into the prepared pan. Arrange the pears evenly over the batter. Sprinkle with the pine nut mixture.

Bake for 45 minutes or until a wooden pick inserted into the center comes out clean. Cool completely in the pan on a wire rack.

Makes 8 servings

Sesame Chicken Noodle Salad

Ginger spices up this meal, featuring Asian-flavored chicken salad paired with ginger muffins and ginger cookies.

1 (12-ounce) package linguine

1 (6-ounce) package Chinese pea pods

1/2 cup creamy peanut butter

1/4 cup peanut oil or vegetable oil

4 tablespoons soy sauce

3 tablespoons rice vinegar

2 tablespoons brown sugar

1 tablespoon minced fresh ginger root

2 tablespoons sesame oil

1/4 teaspoon cayenne pepper

1 cup shredded carrots

3 cups shredded red cabbage

2 cups roasted, shredded chicken

Cook linguine according to package directions. During the last minute of cooking, add pea pods. Drain; rinse with cold water. Drain again and set aside.

Meanwhile, whisk the peanut butter, peanut oil, soy sauce, vinegar, brown sugar, ginger, sesame oil, and cayenne pepper in a small bowl.

Combine the linguine and pea pods with carrots, the cabbage, and chicken in a large bowl. Pour the peanut sauce over the salad; toss to coat. Refrigerate until serving.

Makes 6 servings

TIPS

To save time, purchase shredded carrots in the produce section of your local supermarket and roasted chicken in the deli. If you are shredding the carrots yourself, use the large holes of your grater or shredder.

To shred cabbage, you can either use the large holes of your grater or cut the cabbage into thin strips with a knife.

Ginger Muffins

2 cups flour

³/₄ teaspoon baking soda

³/₄ teaspoon baking powder

¹/₂ teaspoon salt

6 tablespoons butter, softened

³/₄ cup packed brown sugar

2 eggs

1 cup buttermilk

2 tablespoons grated lemon zest

3 tablespoons minced fresh ginger root

¹/₂ cup coarse gingersnap crumbs

Preheat the oven to 375°F. Spray the muffin cups with cooking spray or use paper liners.

Sift together the flour, baking soda, baking powder, and salt; set aside. Beat the butter and brown sugar in a large bowl with an electric mixer at high speed until well blended. Add the eggs, buttermilk, lemon zest, and ginger; mix well. Add the flour mixture; beat until smooth. Stir in the gingersnap crumbs. Spoon the batter into prepared muffin cups. Bake for 15 minutes or until a wooden pick inserted into the center comes out clean. Cool on a wire rack for 5 minutes; invert to remove muffins from cups. Cool completely on a wire rack.

Makes 12 muffins

Molasses Ginger Cookies

2 cups flour

2 teaspoons baking soda

1 teaspoon cinnamon

¹/₂ teaspoon salt

¹/₂ teaspoon ground cloves

¹/₂ teaspoon ground ginger

³/₄ cup shortening

1 cup sugar

¹/₄ cup molasses

1 egg

¹/₄ cup chopped crystallized ginger

¹/₄ cup sugar

Sift together the flour, baking soda, cinnamon, salt, cloves, and ginger in a bowl; set aside. Melt shortening in a small saucepan over low heat; cool. Beat the shortening, sugar, molasses, and egg in a large bowl with an electric mixer at high speed. Add the flour mixture; stir until combined. Add the crystallized ginger; stir until combined. Cover and refrigerate the dough for at least 2 hours.

Preheat the oven to 375°F. Spray two 15x10¹/₂x1-inch cookie sheets with cooking spray.

Form the dough into 1-inch balls; roll in sugar. Place the balls 2 inches apart on prepared cookie sheets. Bake for 8 to 10 minutes or until lightly browned. Cool on the pans for 10 minutes. Remove to wire racks; cool completely.

Makes 2 ¹/₂ dozen cookies

Southwestern Chicken Cobb Salad

A southwestern twist to the traditional Cobb salad, this version is topped with a creamy chive dressing. Decadent truffle brownies are the perfect ending to the meal.

$^1/_2$ **cup mayonnaise**

$^1/_2$ **cup sour cream**

$^1/_4$ **cup chopped fresh chives**

2 **tablespoons white wine vinegar**

2 **tablespoons minced fresh cilantro**

2 **tablespoons minced fresh flat-leaf parsley**

1 **tablespoon fresh lime juice**

1 **teaspoon sugar**

1 **teaspoon Worcestershire sauce**

$^1/_2$ **teaspoon salt**

$^1/_4$ **teaspoon pepper**

1 **yellow pepper**

1 **red pepper**

4 **boneless, skinless chicken breast halves (4 to 6 ounces each)**

Salt and pepper to taste

1 **(15-ounce) can black beans, rinsed and drained**

2 **tablespoons diced onion**

$^1/_4$ **cup chopped fresh cilantro**

8 **cups chopped romaine lettuce**

4 **hard-cooked eggs, peeled and diced**

2 **ripe avocados, peeled, pitted, and chopped**

2 **tomatoes, chopped**

$^2/_3$ **cup crumbled Queso Añejo cheese**

Whisk together the mayonnaise, sour cream, chives, vinegar, cilantro, parsley, lime juice, sugar, Worcestershire sauce, salt, and pepper in a bowl. Refrigerate, covered, for at least 2 hours.

Prepare a medium-hot fire in a charcoal or gas grill; oil the grill grate with cooking spray. Grill the peppers for 4 to 6 minutes a side, turning once, until they are charred. Place on a plate and cover with plastic wrap; let sit for 20 minutes. Scrape off the charred skin with a knife; cut out the stem. Cut open the peppers and scrape out the veins and seeds with a knife. Cut the peppers into strips; set aside.

Season chicken with salt and pepper. Grill for 6 to 8 minutes a side over medium-high heat until the chicken is firm and no longer pink in the center; cut into $^1/_2$-inch pieces.

Combine the black beans, onion, and cilantro in a bowl; mix well.

Divide the lettuce among 4 dinner plates. Arrange the eggs, avocados, peppers, chicken, tomatoes, black bean mixture, and cheese on top of the lettuce. (*For a nice presentation, assemble the ingredients in rows in the order listed.*)

Pour the dressing over the salad.

Makes 4 servings

NOTE

Queso Añejo is an aged, mild tasting, salty, white cheese found in the specialty cheese section of your local supermarket. It is used primarily as a garnish, crumbled or grated over a variety of dishes. Romano cheese can be substituted.

Mexican Corn Muffins

1 1/4 **cups flour**

3/4 **cup yellow cornmeal**

1/2 **teaspoon salt**

1 **tablespoon baking powder**

1 **teaspoon sugar**

1 **egg, lightly beaten**

1 **cup milk**

1/4 **cup vegetable oil**

1 **(10.75-ounce) can condensed nacho cheese soup**

1 **(11-ounce) can whole kernel corn with red and green peppers, drained**

Preheat the oven to 400°F. Spray muffin cups with cooking spray.

Combine the flour, cornmeal, salt, baking powder, and sugar in a large bowl; set aside. Whisk the egg, milk, oil, and soup in a medium bowl until smooth. Add the corn; stir to combine. Add the corn mixture to the flour mixture; mix by hand until combined. Spoon the batter into prepared muffin cups. Bake for 18 to 20 minutes or until a wooden pick inserted into the center comes out clean. Cool on a wire rack for 5 minutes; invert to remove muffins from cups. Serve warm.

Makes 12 muffins

Strawberry Truffle Brownies

3/4 **cup (1 1/2 sticks) unsalted butter**

4 **ounces semisweet baking chocolate, chopped**

3 **eggs**

1 **cup sugar**

1/2 **cup strawberry preserves**

3 **tablespoons crème de cassis or other berry-flavored liqueur**

1 **cup flour**

1/4 **teaspoon salt**

1 **cup semisweet chocolate chips**

Confectioners' sugar, for dusting

Makes 16 brownies

Preheat the oven to 350°F. Spray a 9x9x2-inch baking pan with cooking spray.

Melt the butter and baking chocolate in a large saucepan over low heat, stirring constantly. Remove from the heat; set aside to cool slightly.

Whisk the eggs in a medium bowl. Add the sugar, preserves, and liqueur; mix well. Pour into the chocolate mixture and blend well. Add the flour and salt; mix well. Stir in the chocolate chips. Pour into the prepared pan.

Bake for about 45 minutes or until a wooden pick inserted in the center comes out with moist crumbs. Cool completely in the pan on a wire rack. Run a small knife between the brownies and the sides of the pan. Cut into 16 squares. Just before serving, dust the tops with confectioners' sugar.

Spiced Chicken Salad

*Creamy blue cheese dressing covers spicy baked
chicken strips in this scrumptious salad.*

- ¹/₂ **cup sour cream**
- ¹/₂ **cup mayonnaise**
- 4 **tablespoons buttermilk**
- 1 **tablespoon red wine vinegar**
- ¹/₂ **teaspoon Worcestershire sauce**
- ¹/₄ **teaspoon white pepper**
- ¹/₈ **teaspoon hot pepper sauce**
- ¹/₂ **cup crumbled blue cheese**
- 1 **cup bread crumbs**
- ¹/₂ **teaspoon curry powder**
- ¹/₂ **teaspoon ground ginger**
- ¹/₂ **teaspoon salt**
- ¹/₂ **teaspoon ground cumin**
- ¹/₄ **teaspoon ground allspice**
- ¹/₄ **teaspoon cayenne pepper**
- 4 **boneless, skinless chicken breast halves (4 to 6 ounces each), cut into thin strips**
- ¹/₂ **cup buttermilk**
- 1 **(10-ounce) package Italian salad greens**
- 2 **Granny Smith apples, cored and sliced**
- ¹/₄ **cup walnut halves, toasted**

Preheat the oven to 400°F. Spray a 13x9x2-inch baking dish with cooking spray.

Whisk together the sour cream, mayonnaise, 4 tablespoons buttermilk, vinegar, Worcestershire sauce, white pepper, and hot pepper sauce in a small bowl; stir in the cheese. Cover and refrigerate.

Combine the bread crumbs, curry, ginger, salt, cumin, allspice, and cayenne pepper in a resealable plastic bag. Dip the chicken into ¹/₂ cup buttermilk; place the chicken in the plastic bag and seal. Shake the bag to coat the chicken with the bread crumb mixture. Place the chicken in the prepared baking dish. Bake for 18 to 20 minutes or until chicken is no longer pink in the center.

Divide the greens among 4 dinner plates; top with the apples, walnuts and chicken strips. Pour the dressing over the salad.

Makes 4 servings

Buttermilk Biscuits

2 ¼ cups sifted flour

2 teaspoons baking powder

1 teaspoon sugar

³/₄ teaspoon salt

¹/₂ teaspoon baking soda

6 tablespoons butter, cold and cut into small pieces

1 cup buttermilk

Preheat the oven to 450°F. Spray a 15x10¹/₂x1-inch baking sheet with cooking spray.

Combine the flour, baking powder, sugar, salt, and baking soda in a large bowl. Cut in the butter with a pastry blender or 2 knives until the mixture resembles coarse crumbs. Add the buttermilk, stirring with a fork. The dough will be very dry and crumbly. Finish incorporating the butter and buttermilk into the dry ingredients by kneading lightly with your hand. Work quickly and don't over-mix.

Turn the dough out onto a lightly floured surface. Gently pat the dough to a 1-inch thickness. Cut out biscuits with a 2-inch round biscuit cutter. Gather and reshape the scraps to a 1-inch thickness. Cut out biscuits to make a total of 12. Place the biscuits 1 inch apart on the prepared baking sheet. Bake for 10 to 15 minutes or until a wooden pick inserted into the center comes out clean. Cool on a wire rack. Serve warm.

Makes 12 biscuits

TIPS

For flaky biscuits, combine ingredients quickly and don't over-mix.

Baked biscuits can be frozen for up to one month.

Tequila and Lime Marinated Chicken Salad

Margaritas go well with this south-of-the-border salad.

$^1/_2$ cup fresh lime juice

3 tablespoons tequila

1 teaspoon ground cumin

1 teaspoon chili powder

4 boneless, skinless chicken breast halves (6 to 8 ounces each)

$^1/_4$ cup fresh lime juice

3 tablespoons chopped fresh cilantro

1 tablespoon tequila

1 teaspoon sugar

$^1/_4$ teaspoon salt

$^1/_8$ teaspoon pepper

$^1/_2$ cup extra-virgin olive oil

1 large fresh tomato, diced

1 small red pepper, thinly sliced

1 small yellow pepper, thinly sliced

1 small red onion, thinly sliced

1 ripe avocado, peeled and diced

1 cup cooked fresh corn kernels or frozen corn kernels, thawed

4 cups red leaf lettuce, shredded

4 cups napa cabbage, shredded

$^1/_2$ cup crumbled tortilla chips

1 cup crumbled Queso Añejo cheese

Combine $^1/_2$ cup lime juice, 3 tablespoons tequila, cumin, and chili powder in a resealable plastic bag; add chicken. Seal bag; turn to coat chicken. Refrigerate for at least 30 minutes; discard the marinade.

Prepare a medium-hot fire in a charcoal or gas grill; oil the grill grate with cooking spray. Grill the chicken for 6 to 8 minutes a side over medium-high heat until the chicken is firm and no longer pink in the center; cut into thin slices.

Combine $^1/_4$ cup lime juice, cilantro, 1 tablespoon tequila, sugar, salt, and pepper in a small bowl; whisk in the oil.

Combine the tomato, peppers, onion, avocado, corn, lettuce, and cabbage in a large bowl. Pour the dressing over the salad; toss to coat. Sprinkle with the tortilla chips and cheese; top with the chicken slices.

Makes 4 servings

Tequila and Lime Marinated Chicken Salad

Guacamole and Chips

Iced Lemon Cookies (see recipe on page 67)

Guacamole and Chips

4 ripe avocados, peeled and pitted

2 small tomatoes, seeded and finely chopped

2 tablespoons fresh lime juice

2 tablespoons chopped fresh cilantro

1 tablespoon minced onion

1/2 teaspoon salt

1/4 teaspoon pepper

Tortilla chips

Mash the avocados with a fork in a large bowl. Add the remaining ingredients and mix well. Serve with tortilla chips.

Makes 3 1/2 cups

TIPS

To help prevent guacamole from turning brown, press an avocado pit into the center of the guacamole. Cover the container tightly with plastic wrap, pressing the wrap down into the bowl to form a protective "skin" over the guacamole. Store in the refrigerator.

Homemade guacamole is so good, but if you are short of time, you can purchase prepared guacamole at your supermarket.

To spice up your homemade or purchased guacamole, add a few drops of hot pepper sauce.

Grilled Turkey Tenderloin Salad

Grilled turkey tenderloins cook quickly and are a different way to enjoy turkey.

2 **red peppers**

3 **tablespoons Dijon mustard**

1 **pound turkey breast tenderloins**

1 **pound cherry tomatoes, rinsed**

1 **pound large whole mushrooms, cleaned**

1 **red onion, cut into quarters**

6 **tablespoons white wine vinegar**

4 **teaspoons honey mustard**

2 **teaspoons olive oil**

6 **cups mixed salad greens**

Prepare a medium-hot fire in a charcoal or gas grill; oil the grill grate with cooking spray. Grill the peppers for 4 to 6 minutes a side, turning once, until they are charred. Place on a plate and cover with plastic wrap; let sit for 20 minutes. Scrape off the charred skin with a knife; cut out the stem. Cut open the peppers and scrape out the veins and seeds with a knife. Cut the peppers into strips; set aside.

Spread the Dijon mustard over the turkey. Grill the turkey for 20 to 25 minutes over medium-high heat, turning occasionally, until the meat is firm and no longer pink in the center. Cut the turkey into 1/2-inch-thick slices; keep warm.

Thread the cherry tomatoes, mushrooms, and onions onto 5 or 6 skewers; grill for 4 to 5 minutes, turning to cook evenly and to prevent charring.

Whisk the vinegar, honey mustard, and oil in a small bowl. Place the greens in a large salad bowl. Pour the dressing over the greens; toss to coat. Divide the salad among 4 dinner plates; top with the grilled vegetables and turkey slices.

Makes 4 servings

Grilled French Bread

1 **mini-loaf French bread (about 12 inches long)**

3 **tablespoons butter, softened**

1 **tablespoon honey**

Cut bread sharply on the diagonal into $1/2$-inch-thick slices that are approximately $2^1/2$ inches wide by 7 inches long. Combine the butter and honey in a small bowl. Spread the butter on both sides of the bread slices. Place the buttered bread on the hot grate of a charcoal or gas grill and grill for 1 to 2 minutes a side or until golden brown. Watch bread carefully as it burns easily.

Makes about 8 slices

Pumpkin Bars

Crust

$1/2$ **cup flour**

$1/2$ **cup rolled oats**

$1/2$ **cup chopped pecans**

$1/4$ **cup packed brown sugar**

$1/4$ **cup melted butter**

1 **teaspoon vanilla extract**

$1/2$ **teaspoon cinnamon**

Filling

$3/4$ **cup sugar**

$1/2$ **teaspoon salt**

1 **teaspoon cinnamon**

$1/2$ **teaspoon ground ginger**

$1/4$ **teaspoon ground nutmeg**

2 **eggs**

1 **(15-ounce) can pure pumpkin**

1 **(12-ounce) can evaporated milk**

Preheat the oven to 350°F. Spray an 8x8x2-inch baking pan with cooking spray.

To make the crust: Combine all of the crust ingredients in a medium bowl; mix well. Press into the bottom of the prepared pan. Bake for 10 minutes; cool on a wire rack for 5 minutes.

To make the filling: Combine the sugar, salt, cinnamon, ginger, and nutmeg in a small bowl. Beat eggs and pumpkin in a large bowl with an electric mixer at medium speed until well blended. Add the sugar mixture; beat to combine. Gradually stir in the milk. Spread the batter over the crust. Bake for 1 hour or until a wooden pick inserted into the center comes out clean. Cool completely on a wire rack.

Makes 16 bars

Honey Mustard Pecan Turkey Salad

Pecans abound in this scrumptious meal—pecan-crusted turkey breast slices, pecan muffins, and cherry pecan bars.

1 ½ cups bread crumbs

½ cup grated Parmesan cheese

3 tablespoons butter, melted

½ teaspoon salt

¼ teaspoon pepper

6 baby Portobello mushroom caps

3 egg whites

2 tablespoons Dijon mustard

1 (17.6-ounce) package turkey breast slices

2 to 4 tablespoons olive oil

¼ cup honey

3 tablespoons white wine vinegar

2 tablespoons coarse-grain brown mustard

½ teaspoon minced garlic

½ cup extra-virgin olive oil

8 cups torn red leaf lettuce

Preheat the oven to 400°F. Spray a 13x9x2-inch baking dish with cooking spray.

Combine the bread crumbs, cheese, butter, salt, and pepper in a shallow dish. Spoon 1 tablespoon bread crumb mixture over each mushroom; reserve remaining bread crumb mixture. Place the mushrooms in a single layer in the prepared baking dish. Bake for 15 to 20 minutes or until mushrooms are tender and topping is browned.

Whisk the egg whites and Dijon mustard in a small bowl. Dip the turkey into the egg mixture; dredge in remaining bread crumb mixture. Working in batches, cook the turkey in the olive oil in a large skillet over medium heat for 2 to 3 minutes a side or until golden brown; keep warm.

Combine the honey, vinegar, brown mustard, and garlic in a small bowl; whisk in the extra-virgin olive oil.

Place the lettuce in a large salad bowl. Pour the dressing over the lettuce; toss to coat. Divide the salad among 6 dinner plates; top with the turkey slices. Place a mushroom cap on the side of each plate.

Makes 6 servings

TIP

Packaged turkey breast slices are now readily available. Ask your butcher if you don't see them in the refrigerated section of the meat department.

Pecan Muffins

2 cups coarsely broken pecans

1 1/2 cups flour

2 teaspoons baking powder

1/4 teaspoon salt

1/8 teaspoon ground allspice

1/2 cup butter, melted

1/2 cup packed brown sugar

1/3 cup milk

1/4 cup maple syrup

1 egg

1 teaspoon vanilla extract

2 tablespoons packed brown sugar

Preheat the oven to 375°F. Spray muffin cups with cooking spray or use paper liners.

Place the pecans on a baking sheet and toast in the oven for 10 to 12 minutes or until lightly browned. Cool on a wire rack.

Sift together the flour, baking powder, salt, and allspice. Add 1 3/4 cups pecans; stir. Set aside. Beat the butter, 1/2 cup brown sugar, milk, maple syrup, egg, and vanilla in a large bowl with an electric mixer at high speed until well blended. Add the butter mixture to the flour mixture; stir just until combined. Spoon the batter into the muffin cups.

Combine 1/4 cup pecans and 2 tablespoons brown sugar in a small bowl; sprinkle over the batter. Bake for 20 minutes or until a wooden pick inserted into the center comes out clean. Cool on a wire rack for 10 minutes. Serve warm.

Makes 12 muffins

Turkey and Wild Rice Salad

*This easy recipe offers a delicious new way to use up leftover turkey.
Paired with brown bread muffins and pumpkin bars it's
a great way to extend Thanksgiving!*

2 cups cooked shredded turkey

2 cups cooked wild rice

1 cup red seedless grapes, cut into halves

1 red pepper, diced

2 celery stalks, diced

1/2 cup dried cherries

1/2 cup chopped pecans, toasted

4 green onions, chopped

3 tablespoons extra-virgin olive oil

3 tablespoons currant jelly

2 tablespoons fresh lemon juice

2 tablespoons sour cream

1/4 teaspoon salt

Combine the turkey, wild rice, grapes, pepper, celery, dried cherries, pecans, and onions in a large bowl. Whisk the oil, jelly, lemon juice, sour cream, and salt in a small bowl. Pour over the salad; toss to coat.

Makes 4 servings

NOTE

Wild rice is not really rice—it is a long-grain marsh grass grown in North America. It has long, slender brown-black grains that have a nutty flavor and chewy texture. It takes longer to cook than most types of rice—40-60 minutes. You can find cooked wild rice on the shelf in the rice section of your local supermarket.

Boston Brown Bread Muffins

$^1/_2$ **cup rye flour**

$^1/_2$ **cup whole wheat flour**

$^1/_2$ **cup yellow cornmeal**

1 $^1/_2$ **teaspoons baking soda**

$^3/_4$ **teaspoon salt**

1 **cup buttermilk**

1 **egg**

$^1/_3$ **cup packed brown sugar**

$^1/_3$ **cup vegetable oil**

$^1/_3$ **cup molasses**

1 **cup golden raisins**

Preheat the oven to 400°F. Spray muffin cups with cooking spray.

Combine the flours, cornmeal, baking soda, and salt in a large bowl; set aside. Beat the buttermilk, egg, sugar, oil, and molasses in a medium bowl with an electric mixer until combined. Add the milk mixture to the flour mixture and stir with an electric mixer until combined. Add the raisins; mix well. Pour the batter into the prepared muffin cups, filling to the top of the cup. Bake for 15 minutes or until a wooden pick inserted into the center comes out clean. Remove to a wire rack; cool for 5 to 10 minutes. Serve warm.

Makes 12 muffins

Smoked Turkey Salad

This flavorful salad is so easy to make and so delicious,
it's perfect for a picnic or other outdoor gathering.

<table>
<tr><td>*Menu*</td><td>*Smoked Turkey Salad* • *Banana Bread* (See recipe on page 89)
Cranberry Blondies</td></tr>
</table>

1/3 **cup mayonnaise**

3 **tablespoons minced
fresh parsley**

3 **cups diced smoked turkey
breast**

3/4 **cup diced celery**

2 **tablespoons minced onions**

1/2 **cup dried cherries**

1/2 **cup chopped walnuts, toasted**

Whisk the mayonnaise and parsley in a small bowl; set aside. Combine the turkey, celery, onions, dried cherries, and walnuts in a large bowl. Add the mayonnaise mixture and toss to coat. Served chilled.

Makes 4 servings

TIP

Purchase several 1/4-inch-thick slices of smoked deli turkey breast and cut them into cubes.

Cranberry Blondies

1 1/4 **cups flour**

1/2 **teaspoon baking powder**

1/8 **teaspoon salt**

1 **cup packed brown sugar**

6 **tablespoons butter, softened**

1 **egg**

2 **teaspoons vanilla extract**

1 **cup dried cranberries**

Preheat the oven to 350°F. Spray an 8x8x2-inch baking pan with cooking spray.

Sift together the flour, baking powder, and salt; set aside. Beat the brown sugar and butter in a large bowl with an electric mixer at high speed until well blended. Add the egg and vanilla; beat well. Gradually add the flour mixture, beating at low speed just until combined. Stir in the dried cranberries by hand. Spread evenly in the prepared pan.

Bake for 30 to 35 minutes or until a wooden pick inserted into the center comes out clean. Cool completely in the pan on a wire rack. Cut into 16 squares.

Makes 16 blondies

Meat

Beef

Pork

Asian Steak Salad

Flavors abound in this salad—including a ginger and garlic rub on the flank steak and a lime and cilantro vinaigrette dressing made with peanut oil.

$1/3$ cup fresh lime juice

$1/4$ cup chopped fresh cilantro

3 tablespoons soy sauce

2 tablespoons granulated sugar

1 teaspoon minced fresh garlic

$1/8$ teaspoon pepper

3 tablespoons peanut oil

1 tablespoon minced fresh ginger root

2 teaspoons minced fresh garlic

1 tablespoon brown sugar

1 tablespoon soy sauce

$1/4$ teaspoon pepper

$1^1/2$ pounds flank steak

1 large head bok choy

1 head Boston lettuce

1 medium cucumber, peeled, quartered lengthwise, seeded, and sliced

1 (8-ounce) can sliced water chestnuts, drained

1 (8.75-ounce) can whole baby sweet corn, drained and cut in half

$1/2$ small red onion, thinly sliced

1 (3-ounce) can rice noodles

Combine the lime juice, cilantro, 3 tablespoons soy sauce, granulated sugar, 1 teaspoon garlic, and $1/8$ teaspoon pepper in a medium bowl. Add the oil and whisk until blended; set aside.

Stir the ginger, 2 teaspoons garlic, brown sugar, 1 tablespoon soy sauce, and $1/4$ teaspoon pepper in a small bowl to form a paste. Rub 1 tablespoon of the paste on one side of the steak. Prepare a medium-hot fire in a charcoal or gas grill; oil the grill grate with cooking spray.

Grill the steak, rub side down, over medium-high heat for 5 to 6 minutes. Rub remaining paste on top of the steak; flip. Grill the steak for another 5 to 6 minutes or until the meat reaches desired doneness (medium-rare is very pink in the center; medium is light pink in the center; well-done is brown throughout). Remove the meat from the grill and keep warm.

Trim off the white stem end of the bok choy; cut the bok choy into $1/4$-inch-thick pieces. Tear the Boston lettuce into bite-size pieces. Combine the bok choy, lettuce, cucumber, water chestnuts, corn, and red onion. Pour $3/4$ cup of the dressing over the salad; toss to coat.

Cut the steak on the diagonal against the grain into thin slices. Divide the salad among 6 dinner plates; sprinkle with the rice noodles and top with the steak slices. Drizzle the steak slices with the remaining dressing.

Makes 6 servings

Caramelized Pineapple Parfaits

Chocolate Sauce

- 1 (15-ounce) can sweetened cream of coconut
- 6 tablespoons unsweetened cocoa
- $1/2$ teaspoon vanilla extract
- $1/2$ teaspoon coconut extract

Pineapple

- 4 tablespoons ($1/2$ stick) butter
- 1 ripe pineapple, peeled, cored, and cut into $1/4$-inch chunks
- $1/2$ cup packed brown sugar
- $1/2$ cup dark rum
- $1 1/2$ pints vanilla ice cream
- 6 maraschino cherries, drained

To make the sauce: Combine the cream of coconut and cocoa in a heavy, medium saucepan. Heat to a simmer over medium-low heat, whisking until smooth. Remove from the heat. Stir in the vanilla and coconut extract. Cool to room temperature.

To prepare the pineapple: Melt the butter in a large skillet over medium-high heat. Add the pineapple. Cook for 8 to 10 minutes or until well browned on both sides. Add the brown sugar. Cook until the sugar dissolves. Remove the pan from the heat and add the rum. Return the skillet to the heat. Simmer for 3 minutes or until the sauce thickens, scraping any caramelized pineapple from the bottom of the pan.

Divide the pineapple and rum sauce among 6 sundae dishes. Top each serving with a scoop of ice cream, chocolate sauce, and a maraschino cherry.

Makes 6 servings

Beef and Broccoli Salad

Deli roast beef and fresh vegetables tossed with a soy dressing makes a quick, delicious, and healthy meal.

$1/4$ cup extra-virgin olive oil

$1/4$ cup white wine vinegar

2 tablespoons soy sauce

1 tablespoon sugar

$1/4$ teaspoon pepper

$1/8$ teaspoon ground cloves

$1/8$ teaspoon cinnamon

2 cups broccoli florets

1 cup shredded carrot

1 (8.75-ounce) can whole baby sweet corn, drained

6 cups torn romaine lettuce

$1/2$ pound lean cooked deli roast beef, cut into thin strips

1 cup sliced fresh mushrooms

1 cup chow mein noodles

Whisk together the oil, vinegar, soy sauce, sugar, pepper, cloves, and cinnamon in a small bowl; set aside.

Place the broccoli and carrots in a steamer basket. Place the basket in a saucepan over 1 inch of water; bring to a boil. Cover and steam for 5 minutes or until crisp-tender; drain and set aside to cool.

Combine broccoli, carrots, corn, lettuce, roast beef, and mushrooms in a large bowl. Pour the dressing over the salad; toss to coat. Divide the salad among 4 dinner plates. Sprinkle the salad with the noodles just before serving.

Makes 4 servings

TIP

Purchasing pre-cut and washed broccoli florets, sliced mushrooms, and shredded carrots in the produce section of your supermarket makes the preparation even faster for this salad.

NOTE

For a fast dessert, use the leftover chow mein noodles to make the Chocolate Crunchies.

Apricot Oatmeal Muffins

1 (15-ounce) can apricot halves
1 cup all-purpose flour
1/2 cup whole wheat flour
1/2 cup old-fashioned oats
1/2 cup chopped dried apricots
1/4 cup sugar
2 teaspoons baking powder
1 teaspoon baking soda
1/2 teaspoon salt
1 egg
1 teaspoon vanilla extract

Preheat the oven to 400°F. Spray muffin cups with cooking spray.

Drain the canned apricots, reserving juice. Process the drained apricots in a blender or food processor until puréed. Combine the flours, oats, dried apricots, sugar, baking powder, baking soda, and salt in a large bowl. In another bowl, stir the apricot purée, 1/4 cup reserved apricot juice, egg, and vanilla until combined. Add the apricot mixture to the flour mixture; stir by hand until blended. Spoon the batter into the prepared muffin cups. Bake for 15 to 18 minutes or until a wooden pick inserted into the center comes out clean. Cool in the pan on a wire rack for 5 minutes. Remove the muffins from the pan. Cool completely on a wire rack.

Makes 12 muffins

Chocolate Crunchies

1 cup semisweet chocolate chips
1 cup butterscotch chips
1/2 cup chopped salted cashews
2 cups chow mein noodles

Melt the chips in a small heatproof bowl set over a saucepan of simmering water, stirring constantly until smooth. Remove the bowl from the pan; set on a hot pad. Add the cashews and noodles to the chocolate; stir until combined. Drop the mixture by tablespoonfuls onto a waxed paper-lined baking sheet. Let sit at room temperature for at least 15 minutes or refrigerate for about 5 minutes, until set. Store in a covered container.

Makes 1 1/2 dozen

Beef Stir-Fry Salad

Stir-fried beef and vegetables served over napa cabbage is a nice change from the usual rice accompaniment. A creamy peanut butter sauce makes it even more tasty.

$1/4$ cup extra-virgin olive oil

6 teaspoons creamy peanut butter

1 tablespoon soy sauce

2 teaspoons sesame oil

$1/2$ teaspoon salt

$1/4$ teaspoon pepper

1 carrot, thinly sliced

1 small yellow squash, thinly sliced

1 small zucchini, thinly sliced

1 (8-ounce) can sliced water chestnuts, drained

1 teaspoon sesame oil

1 pound boneless sirloin beef or top round steak, cut into thin strips

1 tablespoon minced fresh ginger root

1 teaspoon minced fresh garlic

1 teaspoon sesame oil

1 head napa cabbage, cut crosswise into thin strips

4 green onions, minced

Whisk the olive oil, peanut butter, soy sauce, 2 teaspoons sesame oil, salt, and pepper in a small bowl; set aside. Cook carrots in a small amount of boiling water in a small saucepan for 3 minutes; drain.

Stir-fry squash, zucchini, and water chestnuts in 1 teaspoon sesame oil in a large skillet for 2 to 3 minutes or until vegetables are crisp-tender. Remove the vegetables from the pan; keep warm. Stir-fry the beef, ginger, and garlic in 1 teaspoon sesame oil for about 5 minutes or until the meat is slightly pink in the center. Add the peanut butter mixture; stir to combine.

In a large bowl, combine the cabbage, carrots, stir-fried vegetables, and beef; toss to combine. Sprinkle with the green onions.

Makes 4 servings

TIP

Napa cabbage, otherwise known as Chinese cabbage, has white ribs and veiny green leaves. It's commonly used in Asian cooking and can be found year-round in the produce section of your local supermarket.

Whole Wheat Rolls

Purchase whole wheat rolls to warm in the oven or serve another easy-to-prepare bread. Or, make the Honey Whole Wheat Dinner Rolls on page 3.

Pear and Dried Cranberry Crisp

Topping

- 1/3 **cup oatmeal**
- 2 **tablespoons brown sugar**
- 1/4 **teaspoon cinnamon**
- 3 **tablespoons butter, cold and cut into small pieces**
- 1/3 **cup flaked coconut**
- 1/3 **cup sliced almonds**

Filling

- 1/2 **cup dried cranberries**
- 5 **teaspoons orange marmalade**
- 1 **tablespoon sugar**
- 1/4 **teaspoon ground allspice**
- 1/4 **teaspoon almond extract**
- 4 **Anjou or Bosc pears, peeled, cored, and sliced**

Preheat the oven to 350°F. Spray four 8-ounce ramekins with cooking spray.

To make the topping: Combine the oatmeal, brown sugar, and cinnamon in a small bowl. Cut in the butter with a pastry blender or 2 knives until the mixture resembles coarse crumbs. Stir in the coconut and almonds; set aside.

To make the filling: Combine the dried cranberries, orange marmalade, sugar, allspice, and almond extract in a bowl. Add the pears; toss gently to coat. Spoon into the prepared ramekins. Sprinkle the topping evenly over the fruit, lightly pressing it in place. Bake for 20 to 25 minutes or until the filling is bubbling. Serve warm or at room temperature.

Makes 4 servings

TIP

Assemble all of the ingredients in the ramekins before dinner and bake the crisp while you eat.

Beef Salsa Salad

Salsa vinaigrette is just the right dressing for grilled flank steak seasoned with south-of-the-border spices.

3 tablespoons extra-virgin olive oil

2 tablespoons fresh lime juice

3 tablespoons prepared salsa

1 tablespoon Mexican seasoning

1½ pounds flank steak or boneless sirloin steak

8 cups torn mixed greens

2 medium tomatoes, coarsely chopped

1 avocado, peeled, pitted, and diced

1 (4.25-ounce) can chopped ripe olives

1 cup fresh corn kernels or frozen corn kernels, thawed

1 cup shredded Cheddar cheese

Whisk together the oil, lime juice, and salsa in a small bowl; set aside.

Prepare a medium-hot fire in a charcoal or gas grill; oil the grill grate with cooking spray. Sprinkle half of the Mexican seasoning on one side of the steak. Grill the steak, seasoned side down, over medium-high heat for 5 to 6 minutes. Rub the remaining seasoning on top of the steak; flip. Grill the steak for another 5 to 6 minutes or until the meat reaches desired doneness (medium-rare is very pink in the center; medium is light pink in the center; well-done is brown throughout). Remove the meat from the grill and keep warm.

Combine the greens, tomatoes, avocado, olives, corn, and cheese in a large bowl; toss to combine. Pour the dressing over the salad; toss to coat. Cut the steak into thin slices. Divide the salad among 4 dinner plates; top with the steak slices.

Makes 4 servings

TIP

Serve salad with tortilla chips and additional salsa.

Banana Chocolate Bars

2 cups flour

1 cup old-fashioned oats

1 tablespoon baking powder

3/4 teaspoon salt

1 cup (2 sticks) butter, softened

1 cup granulated sugar

1 cup packed brown sugar

2 eggs

2 very ripe bananas, mashed

2 teaspoons vanilla extract

1 (11.5-ounce package) semi-sweet chocolate chunks

1 cup walnuts, toasted and chopped

Preheat the oven to 350°F. Spray a 13x9x2-inch baking pan with cooking spray.

Combine the flour, oats, baking powder, and salt in a medium bowl; set aside.

Beat the butter and sugars in a large bowl with an electric mixer at high speed until fluffy. Add the eggs, one at a time, beating well after each addition. Beat in the bananas and vanilla. Gradually add the flour mixture, beating at low speed just until combined. Stir in the chocolate chunks and walnuts by hand. Spread the batter evenly in the prepared pan.

Bake for 45 minutes or until a wooden pick inserted into the center comes out clean. Cool completely in the pan on a wire rack. Cut into 24 bars.

Makes 2 dozen bars

Beef Tortellini Salad

Assemble this meal in the morning and refrigerate it during your busy day so that dinnertime is a snap.

1 (9-ounce) package refrigerated spinach tortellini

1 tablespoon olive oil

1 pound boneless sirloin steak, cut into thin strips

1 zucchini, peeled and cut into small chunks

1 (7.5-ounce) jar marinated artichoke hearts

½ cup thinly sliced roasted red peppers

2 cups halved cherry tomatoes

1 cup cubed mozzarella cheese

1 tablespoon minced fresh parsley

2 tablespoons minced fresh basil

⅓ cup extra-virgin olive oil

3 tablespoons balsamic vinegar

½ teaspoon dried thyme

½ teaspoon dried oregano

1 garlic clove, minced

Prepare tortellini according to package directions; drain. Heat 1 tablespoon olive oil in a large skillet over medium-high heat. Add the beef strips and sauté until slightly pink in the center. Remove the meat with a slotted spoon; cut the strips in half. Combine the tortellini, beef, zucchini, artichoke hearts, peppers, tomatoes, cheese, parsley, and basil in a large bowl. Whisk together ⅓ cup extra-virgin olive oil, vinegar, thyme, oregano, and garlic in a small bowl. Pour the dressing over the salad; toss to coat. Cover and refrigerate for 4 to 8 hours.

Makes 6 servings

TIP

You can substitute any flavor of tortellini—dried or refrigerated—in this recipe. Spinach tortellini can be found in the refrigerated dairy section of your local supermarket.

Italian Tomato Cheese Muffins

2 cups flour

1 tablespoon baking powder

$^1/_4$ teaspoon salt

1 teaspoon Italian seasoning

1 teaspoon dried oregano

$^1/_4$ teaspoon minced fresh garlic

1 cup grated mozzarella cheese

$^1/_4$ cup shredded Parmesan cheese

1 egg, lightly beaten

1 cup milk

5 tablespoons olive oil

1 medium tomato, seeded and chopped

Preheat the oven to 400°F. Spray muffin cups with cooking spray.

Sift together the flour, baking powder, and salt in a large bowl. Add the Italian seasoning, oregano, garlic, and cheeses; stir to combine. Combine the egg, milk, and oil in a small bowl. Add the egg mixture to the flour mixture; stir well. Add the tomato; stir to combine. Spoon the batter into the prepared muffin cups. Bake for 15 minutes or until lightly browned. Cool on a wire rack; serve warm.

Makes 12 muffins

Quick Chiffon Cheesecake

1 cup graham cracker crumbs

2 tablespoons sugar

3 tablespoons butter, melted

1 (8-ounce) package cream cheese, softened

$^1/_2$ cup sugar

1 (10-ounce) jar prepared lemon curd

1 cup frozen whipped topping, thawed

Preheat the oven to 350°F. Spray an 8x8x2-inch baking pan with cooking spray.

Combine graham cracker crumbs, 2 tablespoons sugar, and butter in a small bowl; toss with a fork until the crumbs are moistened. Press the crumb mixture onto the bottom of the prepared pan. Bake for 12 to 15 minutes or until lightly browned. Cool completely on a wire rack.

Beat the cream cheese and $^1/_2$ cup sugar in a large bowl with an electric mixer until smooth. Add the lemon curd; mix until combined. Add the whipped topping; stir to combine. Spread the lemon filling over the crust; smooth the top. Refrigerate for 8 hours or overnight.

Makes 6 servings

Bistro Beef Salad

Easy-to-make herb bread goes well with this quick beef salad. End the meal with a purchased cheesecake served with a brandy cherry sauce.

8 medium red potatoes, cut into quarters

2 tablespoons chopped shallots

2 tablespoons white wine vinegar

2 teaspoons Dijon mustard

1 tablespoon minced fresh parsley

1 tablespoon chopped fresh tarragon or 1 teaspoon dried tarragon

2 tablespoons cold water

1/4 teaspoon salt

1/4 teaspoon freshly ground black pepper

4 tablespoons extra-virgin olive oil

8 cups torn red leaf lettuce

2 cups halved red or yellow cherry tomatoes

4 beef tenderloin steaks (4 ounces each)

2 tablespoons olive oil

Place potatoes in a medium-sized saucepan and cover with water by 1 inch. Bring to a boil over medium heat and cook for 15 minutes or until tender; drain and set aside to cool.

Whisk together shallots, vinegar, mustard, parsley, tarragon, water, salt, and pepper in a small bowl. Add 4 tablespoons extra-virgin olive oil and whisk to combine; set aside.

Divide the lettuce among 4 dinner plates. Arrange the potatoes and tomatoes on one side of each plate.

Cook steaks in 2 tablespoons olive oil in a large skillet for 3 to 5 minutes a side until slightly pink in the center. Place 1 steak on each salad alongside the potatoes and tomatoes. Drizzle the salads with the dressing.

Makes 4 servings

TIP

Quick-cooking beef tenderloin steaks make this salad a snap. You can substitute a larger cut of steak and grill them, if you prefer.

Herbed Wheat Bread

1 (¹/₄-ounce) package active
   dry yeast

³/₄ cup warm milk (110°F to 115°F)

1 cup whole wheat flour

1 egg, lightly beaten

1 tablespoon sugar

¹/₂ teaspoon salt

¹/₄ cup wheat germ

¹/₂ teaspoon dried dill

¹/₂ teaspoon dried thyme

1¹/₄ cups all-purpose flour

1 tablespoon butter, melted

Dissolve the yeast in the warm milk in a large bowl. Add the wheat flour, egg, sugar, and salt; stir with a spoon until combined. Add the wheat germ, dill, thyme, and all-purpose flour; knead with your hands to combine. Turn the dough onto a lightly floured surface and knead for 5 minutes until smooth. Place the dough in a greased bowl, turning once to grease the top of the dough. Cover and let rise in a warm place for 1 hour or until doubled in size. Punch the dough down and place it onto a lightly floured surface; knead 5 to 6 times. Shape the dough into a round loaf. With a sharp knife, cut a 4-inch cross, ¹/₂-inch deep, in the top of the loaf. Spray an 11x17-inch baking sheet with cooking spray. Place the loaf on the prepared baking sheet. Cover and let rise in a warm place for 20 minutes or until doubled in size.

Preheat the oven to 400°F. Brush the loaf with the melted butter. Bake for 18 to 20 minutes or until golden brown. Cool on a wire rack; serve warm.

Makes 1 loaf

Cheesecake with Cherry Sauce

1 (15-ounce) can Bing cherries,
   undrained

¹/₄ cup sugar

2 tablespoons brandy

¹/₄ teaspoon almond extract

1 (30-ounce) package frozen
   New York-style cheesecake,
   thawed

Combine the cherries with their juice, sugar, brandy, and almond extract in a medium saucepan. Cook over medium heat until the sugar dissolves. Serve the warm sauce over the cheesecake.

Grilled Steak Salad
with Blue Cheese Dressing

You can use this tasty blue cheese dressing recipe on any salad.

1/2 cup sour cream

1/2 cup mayonnaise

4 tablespoons buttermilk

1 tablespoon red wine vinegar

1/2 teaspoon Worcestershire sauce

1/4 teaspoon white pepper

1/8 teaspoon hot pepper sauce

1/2 cup crumbled blue cheese

1 pound green beans, trimmed

4 New York strip steaks
   (8 ounces each)

1 teaspoon seasoned salt
   (such as Lawry's)

6 cups torn romaine lettuce

2 medium tomatoes, sliced

Whisk together the sour cream, mayonnaise, buttermilk, vinegar, Worcestershire sauce, pepper, and hot pepper sauce in a small bowl; stir in the cheese. Cover and refrigerate.

Place the beans in a steamer basket. Place the basket in a saucepan over 1 inch of water; bring to a boil. Cover and steam for 5 minutes or until crisp-tender; drain and set aside to cool.

Prepare a medium-hot fire in a charcoal or gas grill; oil the grill grate with cooking spray. Season the steaks with seasoned salt. Grill the steaks for 5 to 6 minutes a side over medium-high heat or until meat reaches desired doneness (medium-rare is very pink in the center; medium is light pink in the center; well-done is brown throughout). Remove the steaks from the grill; cut into thin slices.

Divide the lettuce among 4 dinner plates. Arrange tomato slices and green beans on the lettuce. Drizzle the dressing over the salads. Top with the steak slices.

Makes 4 servings

Bruschetta

8 large plum tomatoes, seeded and diced

10 large fresh basil leaves, cut into thin strips

3 tablespoons shredded fresh Parmesan cheese

3 tablespoons extra-virgin olive oil

$^1/_4$ teaspoon salt

$^1/_8$ teaspoon pepper

16 slices Italian bread, cut $^1/_2$- to $^3/_4$-inch thick

2 garlic cloves, cut in half

Combine the tomatoes, basil, cheese, oil, salt, and pepper in a small bowl. Toast the bread until lightly golden on both sides. While still warm, rub one side of the toast with the cut side of the garlic; top with the tomato mixture.

Makes 3 cups tomato mixture

Strawberries Romanoff

1 (10-ounce) package frozen raspberries in syrup, thawed and undrained

2 pints strawberries, cut into quarters

$^1/_4$ cup Grand Marnier liqueur

3 tablespoons sugar

1 tablespoon fresh lemon juice

1 teaspoon vanilla extract

1 quart vanilla ice cream, softened

Whipped cream, as a garnish

Process the raspberries with their syrup and 1 cup strawberries in a blender or food processor until puréed. Pour through a fine strainer set over a medium bowl to remove the seeds, pressing the purée through the strainer. Discard the seeds in the strainer. Add the liqueur, sugar, lemon juice, and vanilla to the purée; stir to dissolve the sugar. Blend $^1/_2$ cup of the berry mixture with the softened ice cream in a large bowl. Cover; freeze for 1 to 4 hours. Combine the remaining strawberries and the remaining berry purée in a medium bowl; refrigerate until ready to serve.

To serve, divide the strawberry sauce among 6 dessert dishes. Top each with a scoop of strawberry ice cream. Garnish with whipped cream, if desired.

Makes 6 servings

Grilled Steak and Vegetable Salad

An elegant salad meal to serve for company—grilled filet mignon and vegetables glazed with a warm balsamic dressing and served with a goat cheese tart.

¹/₂ cup balsamic vinegar

2 tablespoons sugar

3 tablespoons honey

5 teaspoons soy sauce

2 teaspoons dried thyme

1 teaspoon garlic salt

1 teaspoon coarsely ground black pepper

4 beef tenderloin filet mignon steaks (about 2 pounds)

1 medium onion, sliced

1 zucchini, sliced

1 yellow squash, sliced

1 red pepper, sliced

1 fennel bulb, sliced

1 cup baby carrots, cut into halves lengthwise

2 cups sliced baby bella mushrooms

1 tablespoon olive oil

6 cups chopped romaine lettuce

Combine the vinegar, sugar, honey, and soy sauce in a small saucepan. Bring to a boil over medium heat. Reduce heat and simmer for 8 to 10 minutes or until thickened; set aside. *Reheat just before serving.*

Combine the thyme, garlic salt, and black pepper in a small bowl. Sprinkle over the steaks; rub into both sides. Set aside.

Prepare a medium-hot fire in a charcoal or gas grill; oil the grill grate with cooking spray.

Place the onion, zucchini, squash, red pepper, fennel, carrots, and mushrooms in a grill wok; drizzle with 1 tablespoon oil. Cook and stir for 10 to 15 minutes or until vegetables are crisp-tender; keep warm.

Grill the seasoned steaks for 5 to 6 minutes a side over medium-high heat or until meat reaches desired doneness (medium-rare is very pink in the center; medium is light pink in the center; well-done is brown throughout). Remove the steaks from the grill; cut into thin slices.

Divide the lettuce among 4 dinner plates; top with the vegetables and steak slices. Drizzle the salad with the warm balsamic dressing.

Makes 4 servings

Grilled Steak and Vegetable Salad

Goat Cheese Tart

Grilled Pineapple with Caramel Sauce *(See recipe on page 65)*

Goat Cheese Tart

Crust

1 1/2 **cups flour**

1/2 **teaspoon salt**

6 **tablespoons butter, cold and cut into small pieces**

3 **tablespoons shortening, cold**

4 **tablespoons ice water**

Filling

5 **ounces soft fresh goat cheese**

1/2 **cup heavy cream**

1/4 **cup sour cream**

1/8 **teaspoon salt**

1/8 **teaspoon pepper**

3 **eggs**

1 **tablespoon chopped fresh basil or 1 teaspoon dried basil**

1 **tablespoon chopped fresh dill or 1 teaspoon dried dill**

To make the crust: Process the flour and salt in a food processor until blended. Add the butter and shortening. Pulse until the mixture resembles coarse crumbs. Add the water; pulse just until moist clumps form, adding a little more water, if necessary. Do not overprocess. Gather the dough into a ball; flatten into a disk. Wrap in plastic wrap; refrigerate for 1 hour.

Spray a 9-inch tart pan with a removable bottom with cooking spray. Roll out the dough to a 12-inch circle on a lightly floured surface. Gently lift the dough just enough to move the prepared pan underneath it. Press the dough firmly onto the bottom and side of the pan. If there are places where the dough doesn't reach to the top of the pan, break off any excess dough and press it into place. Reinforce the seam where the bottom and side meet with excess dough. Pierce the bottom of the crust all over with a fork. Cover; freeze for 30 minutes. Preheat the oven to 400°F.

Place the tart pan on a baking sheet. Bake the crust for 20 to 25 minutes or until lightly browned on the bottom. Cool for 5 minutes on a wire rack. *Reduce oven temperature to 375°F.*

To make the filling: Beat the goat cheese, cream, sour cream, salt, and pepper in a large bowl with an electric mixer until blended. Add the eggs, basil, and dill; stir until combined. Pour the filling into the crust. Bake for 20 minutes or until a wooden pick inserted into the center comes out clean. Cool on a wire rack. Serve the tart warm or at room temperature. Refrigerate leftovers.

Makes 6 servings

Mediterranean Beef Salad

Grilled sirloin steak served over tomatoes, cucumbers, grilled onions, toasted pita bread slices, and feta cheese makes a delicious salad any season of the year.

1/4 cup minced fresh mint leaves

1/4 cup minced fresh parsley

2 garlic cloves, chopped

3 tablespoons fresh lemon juice

1 tablespoon white wine vinegar

3 tablespoons extra-virgin olive oil

4 (6- to 7-inch) pita bread rounds, toasted

8 cups torn romaine lettuce

3 medium tomatoes, chopped

1 cucumber, peeled, cut into quarters and sliced

1/2 cup crumbled feta cheese

1 large onion, cut into quarters

1 1/2 pounds boneless sirloin steak

Whisk together the mint, parsley, garlic, lemon juice, vinegar, and oil in a small bowl; set aside.

Slice the toasted pita into thin strips. Combine the pita, lettuce, tomatoes, cucumber, and feta cheese in a large bowl.

Prepare a medium-hot fire in a charcoal or gas grill; oil the grill grate with cooking spray. Thread the onion quarters on 2 skewers; grill for 5 to 10 minutes, turning to cook evenly and to prevent charring. Grill the steak for 5 to 6 minutes a side over medium-high heat or until the meat reaches desired doneness (medium-rare is very pink in the center; medium is light pink in the center; well-done is brown throughout). Remove the steak from the grill; slice into thin strips.

Add the onion to the lettuce mixture. Pour the dressing over the salad; toss to coat. Divide the salad among 4 dinner plates; top with the steak slices.

Makes 4 servings

Mediterranean Beef Salad

Pita with Hummus

Lemon Mousse with Raspberries

Pita with Hummus

1 (15-ounce) can chickpeas or garbanzo beans, drained

1 garlic clove, chopped

2 tablespoons fresh lemon juice

2 tablespoons tahini

$^1/_4$ teaspoon ground cumin

$^1/_8$ teaspoon salt

$^1/_8$ teaspoon pepper

2 tablespoons extra-virgin olive oil

Pita chips or pita bread rounds

Process the chickpeas and garlic in a food processor until smooth. Combine the lemon juice, tahini, cumin, salt, and pepper in a small bowl. Add to the chickpeas; process until smooth. With the processor on, pour the oil through the food chute; process until combined. Store in the refrigerator until ready to use. Serve with pita chips or warm pita bread rounds. To warm pita bread, cut rounds into segments. Place on a baking sheet and broil for 4 to 5 minutes, turning once, until brown.

Makes $^1/_2$ cup

NOTE

Tahini is a smooth, rich paste ground from sesame seeds. It is used in Middle Eastern cooking to enrich the flavor and texture of dishes. Jars and cans of tahini are found in Middle Eastern markets and in the international section of your local supermarket.

Lemon Mousse with Raspberries

1 (10-ounce) jar prepared lemon curd

1 cup heavy cream

2 tablespoons sugar

1 pint fresh raspberries

Whisk the lemon curd in a medium bowl for 2 minutes or until smooth. Beat the cream and sugar in a bowl with an electric mixer at high speed until soft peaks form. Gently fold the whipped cream into the lemon curd until combined. Do not overmix. A few white streaks of cream may be visible. Cover and refrigerate for at least 2 hours. (Lemon mousse can be made up to 2 days ahead. Store, covered, in the refrigerator.)

Divide the raspberries among 4 dessert bowls. Spoon the mousse over the berries.

Makes 4 servings

Skirt Steak Salad

Chipotle dressing and a spicy rub dress up skirt steak with mushrooms and peppers in this dinner from the grill.

1 tablespoon chili powder

1 teaspoon ground coriander

1 teaspoon salt

1/2 teaspoon ground cumin

1/2 teaspoon garlic powder

1/2 teaspoon onion powder

1/2 teaspoon black pepper

2 pounds skirt steak

2 limes

1/4 cup balsamic vinegar

1/2 cup extra-virgin olive oil

1/4 teaspoon salt

1/4 teaspoon black pepper

4 large portobello mushroom caps

1/2 cup mayonnaise

2 tablespoons coarse-grained mustard

1 tablespoon white wine vinegar

3 tablespoons prepared chipotle sauce

1 red pepper

1 green pepper

1/4 cup extra-virgin olive oil

1 tablespoon minced fresh cilantro

1 tablespoon balsamic vinegar

8 cups torn red leaf lettuce

Combine the chili powder, coriander, 1 teaspoon salt, cumin, garlic powder, onion powder, and 1/2 teaspoon black pepper in a small bowl. Rub both sides of the skirt steak with the chili powder mixture. Place in a 15x10x2-inch baking dish; let stand for 10 minutes. Cut the limes in half and squeeze the lime juice over the beef, turning to coat both sides. Cover and refrigerate for 30 to 60 minutes.

Whisk together 1/4 cup balsamic vinegar, 1/2 cup oil, 1/4 teaspoon salt, and 1/4 teaspoon black pepper in a small bowl. Place the mushroom caps, tops up, in an 8x8x2-inch baking dish; pour the marinade over the mushrooms. Move the mushrooms around in the marinade to coat; turn over so caps are facing down. Cover and refrigerate for 30 to 60 minutes.

Whisk together the mayonnaise, mustard, white wine vinegar, and chipotle sauce in a small bowl. Refrigerate until ready to serve.

Prepare a medium-hot fire in a charcoal or gas grill; oil the grill grate with cooking spray. Grill the peppers for 4 to 6 minutes a side, turning once, until they are charred. Place the peppers on a plate and cover with plastic wrap; let sit for 20 minutes. Scrape off the charred skin of the peppers with a knife; cut out the stems. Cut open the peppers and scrape out the veins and seeds with a knife. Cut the peppers into strips; set aside.

Remove the mushrooms from the marinade. Grill the mushrooms, top side up, for 3 minutes. Brush the tops with additional marinade; flip. Grill for 4 to 6 minutes or until caps are tender and browned. Remove the mushrooms from the grill; keep warm.

(continued)

Skirt Steak Salad (cont.)

Remove the skirt steak from the marinade; discard marinade. Grill the steak for 6 to 8 minutes, turning frequently, until meat reaches desired doneness (medium-rare is very pink in the center; medium is light pink in the center; well-done is brown throughout). Remove the steak from the grill and keep warm.

Whisk together 1/4 cup oil, cilantro, and 1 tablespoon balsamic vinegar in a large bowl. Add the lettuce; toss to coat. Divide the lettuce among 4 dinner plates; top with sliced peppers, sliced mushrooms and sliced steak. Drizzle the salads with the chipotle dressing.

Makes 4 servings

TIP

Chipotle sauce can be found in the Mexican section of your local supermarket.

Grilled French Bread

1 **mini-loaf French bread (about 12 inches long)**

3 **tablespoons butter, softened**

Cut the bread in half horizontally. Spread the butter on the cut sides of the bread. Place the bread on a hot grill grate, buttered side down, and grill for 1 to 2 minutes or until golden brown. Cut into halves.

Makes 4 pieces

Grilled Pineapple with Caramel Sauce

1 **fresh pineapple, peeled, cored, and sliced or 1 (8-ounce) can pineapple slices, drained**

Vanilla ice cream or vanilla frozen yogurt

Caramel ice cream topping

Prepare a medium-hot fire in a charcoal or gas grill; oil the grill grate with cooking spray. Grill pineapple slices for 2 to 3 minutes a side, turning once, until golden brown. Divide the hot pineapple slices among 4 or 6 dessert dishes; top with a scoop of ice cream. Drizzle with the caramel sauce.

Makes 4 to 6 servings

Steak Salad with Buttermilk Dressing

This easy salad makes a quick weeknight meal.
Bake tomato bread and cookies as accompaniments
or purchase something already prepared from the supermarket.

³/₄ cup buttermilk

¹/₄ cup mayonnaise

2 tablespoons sour cream

2 tablespoons fresh lemon juice

¹/₂ teaspoon salt

¹/₂ teaspoon onion powder

¹/₄ teaspoon garlic powder

¹/₄ teaspoon white pepper

2 cups sugar snap peas or
Chinese pea pods

1 pound round steak or boneless
sirloin steak

4 teaspoons Worcestershire sauce

2 medium heads Boston lettuce

1 (14-ounce) can hearts of palm,
drained and cut into ¹/₄-inch-
thick slices

2 medium tomatoes,
cut into ¹/₂-inch wedges

1 medium cucumber,
sliced ¹/₄-inch thick

Whisk together the buttermilk, mayonnaise, sour cream, lemon juice, salt, onion powder, garlic powder, and white pepper in a small bowl. Refrigerate until ready to serve.

Cook the peas in 2 cups boiling water in a medium saucepan for 3 to 5 minutes or until crisp-tender; drain. Preheat the broiler; spray the broiler pan rack with cooking spray. Place the steak on the prepared pan; sprinkle with half of the Worcestershire sauce. Broil the steak 4 minutes; turn. Sprinkle with the remaining Worcestershire sauce. Broil for 3 to 4 more minutes or until meat reaches the desired doneness (medium-rare is very pink in the center; medium is light pink in the center; well-done is brown throughout). Cut the steak into thin slices.

Arrange the lettuce, peas, hearts of palm, tomatoes, cucumber, and steak slices on 4 dinner plates. Drizzle the salads with the dressing.

Makes 4 servings

Steak Salad with Buttermilk Dressing

Tomato Bread

Iced Lemon Cookies

Tomato Bread

1 (1-pound) loaf frozen pizza
  dough, thawed

1 egg yolk

1 teaspoon extra-virgin olive oil

2 small tomatoes, sliced

1 teaspoon extra-virgin olive oil

1 teaspoon dried oregano

1/2 teaspoon sugar

1/4 teaspoon freshly ground black
  pepper

Preheat the oven to 400°F. Spray a 15x10x1-inch baking sheet with cooking spray. Stretch the dough to a 10-inch round on the prepared pan; let rest 10 minutes.

Whisk together the egg yolk and 1 teaspoon oil in a small bowl. Brush the dough with the egg wash, leaving a 1/2-inch border around the edge. Bake for 10 minutes; remove to a wire rack. Arrange the tomato slices in overlapping circles on the dough, leaving a 1/2-inch border around the edge. Drizzle with 1 teaspoon oil; sprinkle with the oregano, sugar, and pepper. Bake for 10 to 15 minutes or until golden brown. Cut into wedges.

Makes 6 pieces

Iced Lemon Cookies

Cookies

2 1/4 cups flour

1 teaspoon baking powder

1/2 teaspoon salt

1/2 cup (1 stick) butter, softened

1/2 cup sugar

1/3 cup honey

1 egg

2 teaspoons grated lemon zest

1 teaspoon lemon extract

1/4 cup milk

Icing

1 cup confectioners' sugar, sifted

2 teaspoons grated lemon zest

2 tablespoons fresh lemon juice

Preheat the oven to 350°F. Grease 2 cookie sheets.

To make the cookies: Sift together the flour, baking powder, and salt; set aside. Beat the butter and sugar in a large bowl with an electric mixer at high speed until fluffy. Add the honey, egg, lemon zest, and lemon extract; beat until blended. Add the flour mixture alternately with the milk, beating at medium speed after each addition.

Drop the dough by tablespoonfuls 2 inches apart onto the prepared cookie sheets. Bake for about 12 minutes or until lightly browned. Meanwhile, make the icing.

To make the icing: Whisk together the confectioners' sugar, lemon zest, and lemon juice in a small bowl. Brush over the hot cookies while they are still on the cookie sheets. Remove cookies to wire racks and cool completely.

Makes 3 dozen

Taco Salad

Everyone loves a taco salad. Packaged tortilla shells help simplify the preparation of this popular meal.

1 **pound ground beef**

¹/₄ **cup minced onion**

2 **garlic cloves, minced**

1 **(15-ounce) can black beans, rinsed and drained**

1 **cup frozen corn kernels, thawed**

1 **(8-ounce) jar taco sauce**

1 **tablespoon chili powder**

4 **packaged tortilla shells**

8 **cups chopped iceberg lettuce**

2 **large tomatoes, chopped**

2 **cups shredded Colby-Jack cheese**

1 **cup sour cream**

1 **avocado, peeled and diced**

Cook the beef, onion, and garlic in a large non-stick skillet over medium-high heat for 5 minutes or until meat is no longer pink; drain. Stir in the black beans, corn, taco sauce, and chili powder. Bring to a boil. Reduce heat; cover and simmer for 10 minutes.

Heat the tortilla shells according to the package directions; cool slightly. Fill the shells with the lettuce. Top with the chopped tomatoes and beef mixture. Sprinkle with the cheese. Top with the sour cream and avocado.

Makes 4 servings

TIP

Purchase prepared guacamole in the refrigerated section of the produce section of your local supermarket. Serve it on the side as a dip for the tortilla shell pieces that you break off.

Kahlúa Cream Cheese Brownies

Brownies

- 3/4 **cup (1 1/2 sticks) butter**
- 6 **(1-ounce) squares semisweet chocolate, chopped**
- 3/4 **cup packed light brown sugar**
- 1 **teaspoon vanilla extract**
- 1/4 **teaspoon salt**
- 2 **eggs**
- 3/4 **cup flour**
- 1/2 **cup chopped walnuts**

Topping

- 1 **(8-ounce) package cream cheese, softened**
- 1/2 **cup sugar**
- 2 **tablespoons flour**
- 2 **eggs**
- 3 **tablespoons Kahlúa (or other coffee-flavored liqueur)**
- 1 **teaspoon vanilla extract**
- 1/2 **teaspoon cinnamon**

Preheat the oven to 350°F. Spray a 9x9x2-inch baking pan with cooking spray.

To make the brownies: Melt the butter and chocolate in a small saucepan over low heat, stirring constantly. Add the brown sugar; stir until dissolved. Remove from heat. Add the vanilla and salt. Stir to combine. Add the eggs, one at a time, blending well after each addition. Fold in the flour and nuts. Spread the batter into the prepared pan. Set aside.

To make the topping: Beat the cream cheese, sugar, and flour in a large bowl with an electric mixer at high speed until well blended. Add the eggs, one at a time, beating well after each addition. Add the Kahlúa, vanilla, and cinnamon, beating at medium speed until blended. Spread the topping over the batter.

Bake for 40 to 45 minutes or until the topping is set and lightly browned. Remove to a wire rack; cool in the pan to room temperature. Cover and refrigerate for at least 4 hours. Cut into squares.

Makes 36 bars

TIP

To cut brownies more easily, spray the knife with cooking spray.

Ham and Artichoke Salad

Prepare everything for this meal the night before or earlier in the day. Your dinner is ready to eat when you get home or to take along on a picnic.

2 cups cubed cooked ham

1 ½ cups Monterey Jack cheese, cut into thin strips

1 (14-ounce) can artichoke hearts, drained and cut into halves

1 cup red pepper, cut into thin strips

1 cup green pepper, cut into thin strips

½ cup extra-virgin olive oil

2 tablespoons red wine vinegar

1 tablespoon fresh lemon juice

¼ cup minced fresh parsley

1 teaspoon chopped fresh basil

Combine ham, cheese, artichokes, and peppers in a large bowl. Whisk together oil, vinegar, lemon juice, parsley, and basil in a small bowl. Pour the dressing over the salad; toss to coat. Refrigerate for at least 2 hours before serving.

Makes 4 servings

TIP

You can find cubed ham in the convenience food section in the meat department at your local supermarket. Otherwise, purchase thick-cut deli ham and cut it into cubes.

Ham and Artichoke Salad

Ham and Cheese Muffins

Pineapple and Macadamia Nut Cookies

Ham and Cheese Muffins

1 1/3 cups flour

1 teaspoon baking powder

1/2 teaspoon baking soda

1/2 teaspoon salt

1 egg, beaten

2 tablespoons sugar

1 cup sour cream

1 tablespoon vegetable oil

1 teaspoon prepared mustard

1 cup diced cooked ham

1/2 cup shredded Monterey Jack cheese

Preheat the oven to 400°F. Spray muffin cups with cooking spray.

Sift together the flour, baking powder, baking soda, and salt in a medium bowl; set aside. By hand, stir together egg, sugar, sour cream, oil, and mustard in a large bowl. Add the flour mixture and stir just until moistened. Add the ham and cheese and stir until combined. Spoon the batter into the prepared muffin cups. Bake for 20 to 25 minutes or until a wooden pick inserted into the center comes out clean. Cool in the pan on a wire rack for 10 minutes. Remove the muffins from the pan and cool completely on a wire rack.

Makes 12 muffins

Pineapple and Macadamia Nut Cookies

1 (20-ounce) can crushed pineapple

2 cups flour

1 teaspoon baking soda

1/2 teaspoon baking powder

1/2 cup (1 stick) butter, softened

1 cup packed brown sugar

1 egg

2 cups old-fashioned oats

1/2 cup flaked coconut

1/2 cup macadamia nuts, chopped

1/2 cup white chocolate chips

Preheat the oven to 350°F. Grease 2 cookie sheets.

Drain the pineapple, reserving 2 tablespoons of the juice; set aside. Sift together the flour, baking soda, and baking powder; set aside. Beat the butter and brown sugar in a large bowl with an electric mixer at high speed until well blended. Add the reserved pineapple juice and the egg; beat well. Gradually add the flour mixture and oats, beating at low speed until well blended. Stir in the pineapple, coconut, macadamia nuts, and white chocolate chips by hand.

Drop the dough by rounded teaspoonfuls 2 inches apart onto the prepared cookie sheets. Bake for 13 minutes or until lightly browned. Cool on a wire rack.

Makes 3 dozen cookies

Paella Salad with Sausage

Vegetables and rice make a tasty bed for sausage in this salad,
inspired by traditional Spanish paella.

2 teaspoons olive oil

1 cup chopped onion

1 teaspoon minced fresh garlic

3 cups chicken broth

1/2 teaspoon black pepper

2 cups green beans, trimmed
  and cut into 1-inch pieces

1 cup Arborio rice

1 1/2 cups fresh or frozen corn
  kernels

2 medium zucchini, thinly sliced

1 red pepper, cut into thin strips

1 teaspoon dried basil

2 teaspoons olive oil

6 Italian sausage links

Heat 2 teaspoons oil in a large skillet; add the onion and garlic and sauté until crisp-tender. Add the broth and pepper; bring to a boil. Add the green beans and rice. Return to a boil. Reduce heat; cover and simmer for 8 minutes. Add the corn, zucchini, and red pepper. Cover and cook for 7 to 8 minutes or until rice is tender and liquid is absorbed. Remove from heat; add the basil. Cool to room temperature.

Meanwhile, heat 2 teaspoons oil in a separate skillet and cook sausage over medium heat for about 15 minutes, turning frequently, until sausage is no longer pink. Cut the sausage into thin slices.

Divide the rice mixture among 4 dinner plates; top with the sausage slices.

Makes 6 servings

NOTE

Paella is a Spanish dish that marries vegetables, broth, meat, and fish with short grain rice. Arborio rice is the most widely available short grain rice to use.

Roasted Red Pepper Bread

1 (1-pound) loaf frozen pizza
  dough, thawed

1 egg yolk, beaten

2 teaspoons extra-virgin olive oil

4 large fresh basil leaves, thinly
  sliced

1 (12-ounce) jar roasted red
  peppers, drained

1 teaspoon dried oregano

$^1/_2$ cup finely shredded mozzarella
  cheese

Preheat the oven to 400°F. Spray a 15x10x1-inch baking sheet with cooking spray.

Stretch the dough to a 10-inch round on a lightly floured surface; let rest 10 minutes. Place the dough on the prepared pan. Brush the dough with the egg yolk, leaving a $^1/_2$-inch border around the edge. Bake for 10 minutes; remove the pan to a wire rack. Drizzle the dough with oil; sprinkle with the basil. Arrange the peppers on top, leaving a $^1/_2$-inch border around the edge. Sprinkle with the oregano and cheese. Bake for 10 to 15 minutes or until golden brown. Cut into wedges.

Makes 6 pieces

Lemon Granita

$2^1/_2$ cups water

1 cup sugar

1 cup fresh lemon juice

2 tablespoons grated lemon zest

  Fresh cherries or strawberries,
  as a garnish

Chill a 13x9x2-inch baking pan in the freezer.

Bring the water and sugar to a boil in a large saucepan over medium-high heat, stirring until the sugar dissolves. Remove from the heat; stir in the lemon juice and lemon zest. Let stand, covered, for 10 minutes to infuse the syrup with lemon flavor. Pour through a strainer into the cold baking pan. Cool to room temperature. Cover the pan with foil. Freeze for 1 hour or until ice crystals form around the edges. Stir with a fork to incorporate the ice crystals. Freeze, stirring every 30 minutes, for about 2 hours, until the mixture is slushy with ice crystals throughout.

When ready to serve, run the tines of a fork over the top of the granita to fluff up the ice crystals. Spoon into small dessert dishes. Garnish with cherries or strawberries.

Makes about 1 quart

Grilled Pork Gazpacho Salad

Serving grilled, seasoned pork tenderloin slices on top of fresh tomatoes, peppers, and cucumbers makes a delightful lean meal.

1 teaspoon dried tarragon

1 teaspoon dried oregano

1 teaspoon dried dill

1 teaspoon dried thyme

1 teaspoon garlic powder

2 pork tenderloins
   (1 pound each), trimmed

3 tomatoes, chopped

1 red pepper, diced

1 green pepper, diced

1 yellow pepper, diced

1 cucumber, seeded and diced

1/2 red onion, diced

1 celery stalk, diced

1/4 cup chopped fresh parsley

2 tablespoons red wine vinegar

1 tablespoon extra-virgin olive oil

1/2 teaspoon salt

1/8 teaspoon black pepper

10 cups chopped Romaine lettuce

Combine the tarragon, oregano, dill, thyme, and garlic in a small bowl. Rub the mixture into the pork; place into a 13x9x2-inch baking dish. Refrigerate for 1 hour.

Combine the tomatoes, peppers, cucumber, onion, celery, and parsley in a large bowl. Whisk together the vinegar, oil, salt, and black pepper in a small bowl; pour over the vegetable mixture and toss to coat. Let sit at room temperature for 1 hour.

Prepare a medium fire in a charcoal or gas grill; oil the grill grate with cooking spray. Grill the pork for 20 minutes, turning occasionally, over medium heat until a meat thermometer registers 160°F. Cover and let rest for 5 minutes before cutting. Cut into 1/4-inch-thick slices.

Divide the lettuce among 6 dinner plates. Top with the vegetable mixture and arrange the pork slices on top.

Makes 6 servings

TIPS

Let the tenderloins rest for 5 minutes before cutting to redistribute the juices so the meat is tender and moist. Use this time to grill the bread.

Cutting the pork into thin medallions or thicker steaks also makes a nice presentation.

Grilled French Bread

1 **mini-loaf French bread (about 12 inches long)**

3 **tablespoons butter, softened**

Cut bread in half horizontally. Spread the butter on the cut sides of the bread. Place the bread on a hot grill grate, butter side down, and grill for 1 to 2 minutes or until golden brown. Cut into thirds.

Makes 6 pieces

Peach Sorbet

1 **(20-ounce) package frozen sliced peaches**

¹/₂ **cup sugar**

¹/₈ **teaspoon cinnamon**

Fresh mint leaves, as a garnish

Let the peaches stand at room temperature for 20 minutes or until slightly thawed. Pulse the peaches, sugar, and cinnamon in a food processor several times to break up the fruit. Process continuously until the sugar is dissolved and the peaches are puréed. Transfer to a covered container and freeze for at least 1 hour. (Sorbet can be made up to 3 days ahead.)

Before serving, let the sorbet stand at room temperature for 5 to 10 minutes or until slightly thawed. Spoon into small dessert dishes. Garnish with mint leaves.

Makes 4 servings

TIP

Serve the sorbet in frozen whole peaches for a special presentation. Prepare 4 large peaches as follows: Using a paring knife, cut an almond-shaped opening around the stem end of each peach through to the pit. At the opposite end, poke a skewer into the peach and push the pit out through the opening at the top. Remove the pit gently with your fingers, keeping the peach totally intact. Scoop out the peach flesh, leaving a ¹/₄-inch-thick shell. Brush the inside of each peach with lemon juice. Wrap tightly in plastic wrap and freeze for at least 1 hour. *(Peaches can be prepared up to 3 days ahead.)*

Spiced Grilled Pork Salad

Summer vegetables marinated in tequila and lime juice make a cool bed for spiced grilled pork.

Menu   *Spiced Grilled Pork Salad* • *Sweet Corn Muffins* (See recipe on page 95)
Caramelized Bananas and Ice Cream (See recipe on page 99)

2 cups fresh corn kernels

2 cups diced zucchini

1/4 cup minced red onion

2 teaspoons olive oil

2 cups cherry tomatoes, cut into halves

2 tablespoons minced fresh cilantro

2 tablespoons lime juice

1 tablespoon tequila

1 teaspoon salt

1 tablespoon curry powder

1 teaspoon ground cumin

1 teaspoon salt

1/4 teaspoon cinnamon

2 teaspoons olive oil

1 pork tenderloin (1 pound), trimmed

8 cups torn romaine lettuce

Sauté corn, zucchini, and red onion in 2 teaspoons oil in a large skillet for 4 to 5 minutes or until crisp-tender. Spoon the corn mixture into a large bowl; cool to room temperature. Add tomatoes, cilantro, lime juice, tequila, and 1 teaspoon salt. Toss to coat; set aside.

Combine curry, cumin, 1 teaspoon salt, cinnamon, and 2 teaspoons oil in a small bowl; spread onto pork. Prepare a medium fire in a charcoal or gas grill; oil the grill grate with cooking spray. Grill the pork for 20 minutes, turning occasionally, over medium heat until a meat thermometer registers 160°F. Cover and let rest for 5 minutes before cutting. Cut into 1/4-inch-thick slices.

Add the lettuce to the vegetable mixture; toss to combine. Divide the salad among 4 dinner plates; top with the pork slices.

Makes 4 servings

TIP

To trim tenderloins, cut off any loose fat and the *silverskin*—the connective tissue that has a silver sheen to it.

Seafood/Fish

Crab Pasta Salad

Lump crabmeat, pasta, and tomatoes mixed with a red pepper mayonnaise create a perfect salad for a picnic or a sailing party.

2 **cups uncooked small pasta shells**

2 **(6-ounce) cans lump crabmeat, drained**

1 **cup chopped cherry tomatoes**

¹/₂ **cup diced celery**

¹/₂ **cup mayonnaise**

¹/₄ **cup chopped roasted red peppers**

1 **teaspoon dried dill**

¹/₂ **teaspoon Dijon mustard**

¹/₂ **teaspoon salt**

¹/₄ **teaspoon pepper**

Prepare the pasta according to package directions; drain. Combine pasta, crab, tomatoes, and celery in a large bowl; set aside. Whisk together the mayonnaise, red peppers, dill, mustard, salt, and pepper in a small bowl. Pour the dressing over the pasta mixture; toss to coat. Refrigerate, covered, for at least 1 hour before serving.

Makes 4 servings

TIPS

Canned crab comes in several forms. This recipe calls for lump crab, which is chunks of crabmeat. Cans labeled white crab or crab are shredded pieces of crab.

You can find roasted peppers in the Italian section of your local supermarket.

Granola Muffins

2 cups granola

1 cup flour

1/3 cup packed light brown sugar

2 teaspoons baking powder

1/2 teaspoon salt

1/2 teaspoon cinnamon

1 cup milk

1/3 cup butter, melted

1 egg, lightly beaten

1 teaspoon vanilla extract

1/2 cup golden raisins

1/2 cup flaked coconut

1/3 cup slivered almonds

Preheat the oven to 400°F. Spray muffin cups with cooking spray.

Combine the granola, flour, brown sugar, baking powder, salt, and cinnamon in a large bowl; set aside. Stir together the milk, butter, egg, and vanilla in a small bowl. Add the milk mixture to the flour mixture; stir by hand until combined. Add the raisins, coconut, and almonds; stir to combine. Spoon the batter into the prepared muffin cups. Bake for 15 to 18 minutes or until a wooden pick inserted into the center comes out clean. Cool in the pan on a wire rack for 5 minutes. Remove the muffins from the pan.

Makes 12 muffins

Apple Spice Cookies

2 1/4 cups flour

1 teaspoon cinnamon

1/2 teaspoon baking soda

1/2 teaspoon ground nutmeg

1/2 cup (1 stick) butter, softened

1 cup packed brown sugar

2 eggs

1/4 cup apple juice

1 large Granny Smith apple, peeled, cored, and diced

1 cup pecans, toasted and chopped

Preheat the oven to 375°F. Grease 2 cookie sheets.

Sift together the flour, cinnamon, baking soda, and nutmeg; set aside. Beat the butter and brown sugar in a large bowl with an electric mixer at high speed until well blended. Beat in the eggs and apple juice. Gradually add the flour mixture, beating at low speed until well blended. Stir in the apple and pecans.

Drop the dough by teaspoonfuls 2 inches apart onto the prepared cookie sheets. Bake for 13 minutes or until lightly browned. Cool on a wire rack.

Makes 3 1/2 dozen cookies

Halibut Cobb Salad

Sautéed halibut and vegetables pair up in this tasty new approach to the traditional Cobb salad.

2 pounds halibut, cut into ¹/₂-inch pieces

¹/₂ teaspoon salt

¹/₂ teaspoon pepper

2 tablespoons olive oil

1¹/₂ cups chopped zucchini

1 cup chopped yellow squash

1 tablespoon olive oil

1 large head iceberg lettuce, chopped

2 hard-cooked eggs, peeled and chopped

1 avocado, peeled, pitted and diced

2 ripe tomatoes, chopped

1 cup crumbled blue cheese

¹/₄ cup white wine vinegar

2 tablespoons honey

1 teaspoon dried dill

1 teaspoon salt

¹/₂ teaspoon pepper

6 tablespoons extra-virgin olive oil

Sprinkle halibut with ¹/₂ teaspoon salt and ¹/₂ teaspoon pepper. Cook the halibut in 2 tablespoons olive oil in a large skillet over medium-high heat for 5 to 8 minutes or until fish is opaque. Drain; cool to room temperature. Clean the drippings from skillet.

Cook the zucchini and squash in 1 tablespoon olive oil in the same skillet over medium-high heat for 2 to 3 minutes or until crisp-tender. Cool to room temperature.

Divide the lettuce among 4 dinner plates. Arrange the eggs, avocado, vegetables, tomato, and blue cheese on top of the lettuce. *(For a nice presentation, assemble the ingredients in rows in the order listed.)* Top with the halibut.

Whisk together the vinegar, honey, dill, salt, and pepper in a small bowl. Add the extra-virgin olive oil; whisk until combined. Drizzle the dressing over the salads.

Makes 4 servings

TIP

Halibut—a mild-flavored fish with snowy white flesh—can be purchased as steaks (bone-in) or fillets (boneless pieces of fish).

Whole Wheat Muffins

2 cups whole wheat flour

2 teaspoons baking powder

1 teaspoon baking soda

1 teaspoon cinnamon

$1/4$ teaspoon salt

$1/4$ cup packed dark brown sugar

2 eggs

1 cup buttermilk

$1/4$ cup vegetable oil

2 tablespoons molasses

$1/2$ cup raisins

Preheat the oven to 350°F. Spray muffin cups with cooking spray.

Combine the flour, baking powder, baking soda, cinnamon, salt, and brown sugar in a large bowl; set aside.

Stir together the eggs, buttermilk, oil, and molasses in a small bowl. Add the egg mixture to the flour mixture; stir by hand until combined. Add the raisins; mix to combine. Spoon the batter into the prepared muffin cups. Bake for 18 to 20 minutes or until a wooden pick inserted into the center comes out clean. Cool in the pan on a wire rack for 5 minutes. Remove the muffins from the pan. Store in an airtight container for 1 day to let the flavors develop.

Makes 12 muffins

Poached Salmon
with Cucumber Dressing

Salmon poached in wine makes a light luncheon or dinner salad.

1 cup dry white wine

1 cup water

6 peppercorns

2 bay leaves

1 stalk celery, chopped

1 lemon, sliced

4 salmon fillets (6 ounces each)

1 pound fresh asparagus, trimmed

1/3 cup peeled, seeded, and finely chopped cucumber

1/3 cup sour cream

1/3 cup plain yogurt

2 tablespoons milk

1 teaspoon dried dill

2 teaspoons Dijon mustard

2 teaspoons fresh lemon juice

8 cups chopped romaine lettuce

1 (7.5-ounce) jar marinated artichoke hearts

Combine the wine, water, peppercorns, bay leaves, celery, and lemon in a large skillet; bring to a boil. Reduce heat; cover and simmer for 10 minutes. Add the salmon to the skillet; cover and cook for 10 minutes or until the fish flakes easily when tested with a fork. Transfer the salmon to a platter with a slotted spoon; discard the cooking liquid. Cover the salmon and refrigerate for at least 1 hour or until thoroughly chilled.

Cook the asparagus in a large pot of boiling water for 2 to 3 minutes or until crisp-tender. Drain and rinse under cold water; refrigerate for at least 30 minutes.

Combine the cucumber, sour cream, yogurt, milk, dill, mustard, and lemon juice in a small bowl. Refrigerate until ready to serve.

Divide the lettuce among 4 dinner plates; top with the salmon. Arrange the asparagus and the artichoke hearts alongside the salmon. Pour the dressing over the salads.

Makes 4 servings

Croissants

Purchase ready-made croissants to warm in the oven. Or, purchase refrigerated crescent roll dough and bake as directed.

Poached Pears

4 cups sweet red wine

2 cups water

1 cup sugar

Zest of 1 orange, cut into 3x1-inch strips

1 cinnamon stick

8 whole cloves

4 ripe Bosc pears

¼ cup marscapone cheese, softened

2 tablespoons chopped pistachio nuts

Combine the wine, water, sugar, orange zest, cinnamon stick, and cloves in a non-aluminum stockpot. Bring to a boil, stirring to dissolve the sugar. Meanwhile, peel the pears, keeping the stems intact. Insert a melon baller into the bottom of each pear and twist several times to remove the seeds and core. Cut a thin slice off the bottom of each pear so it stands upright. Add the pears, stem sides up, to the poaching liquid. (To keep the pears submerged in the liquid, cover them with a piece of parchment paper and a plate.) Return to a boil; reduce the heat to low. Simmer, covered, for 45 minutes or until the pears are tender. (A paring knife should pierce the center of the pear without resistance.) Remove the pears with a slotted spoon to a dish. Refrigerate for 2 to 24 hours.

Bring the poaching liquid to a boil; continue boiling for 10 to 15 minutes or until thickened. *(The reduced poaching liquid can be refrigerated for several days. Reheat before serving.)*

Mix the cheese and nuts in a small bowl to combine. Fill the cavity of each chilled pear with the cheese mixture. Stand each pear on a dessert plate. Spoon the warm reduced poaching liquid over the pears. Serve immediately.

Makes 4 servings

Salmon with Red Pepper and Corn

A cool yogurt dressing is drizzled over baked spiced salmon and vegetables in this zesty, colorful salad.

²/₃ **cup plain yogurt**

3 **tablespoons fresh lemon juice**

1 **tablespoon minced fresh parsley**

³/₄ **teaspoon Dijon mustard**

¹/₈ **teaspoon salt**

 Dash white pepper

¹/₂ **teaspoon salt**

¹/₂ **teaspoon ground ginger**

¹/₂ **teaspoon ground coriander**

¹/₄ **teaspoon ground cumin**

¹/₈ **teaspoon black pepper**

4 **salmon fillets (6 ounces each)**

2 **tablespoons fresh lemon juice**

2 **tablespoons olive oil**

2 **tablespoons fresh lemon juice**

2 **tablespoons honey**

1 **red pepper, diced**

1 **cup fresh whole kernel corn or 1 cup frozen whole kernel corn, thawed**

¹/₄ **cup minced red onion**

¹/₄ **cup minced fresh parsley**

 Mixed salad greens

Combine the yogurt, 3 tablespoons lemon juice, 1 tablespoon parsley, mustard, ¹/₈ teaspoon salt, and white pepper in a small bowl. Refrigerate, covered, for at least 30 minutes before serving.

Preheat oven to 425°F. Spray a 13x9x2-inch baking dish with cooking spray.

Combine ¹/₂ teaspoon salt, ginger, coriander, cumin, and black pepper in a small bowl. Place the salmon in the prepared baking dish. Drizzle with 2 tablespoons lemon juice and sprinkle with the seasoning mixture. Bake, uncovered, for 18 to 22 minutes or until fish flakes easily when tested with a fork.

Whisk together 2 tablespoons olive oil, 2 tablespoons lemon juice, and honey in a medium bowl. Add the red pepper, corn, onion, and ¹/₄ cup parsley; toss to coat. Divide the salad greens among 4 dinner plates; top with the red pepper mixture and the salmon fillets. Drizzle the yogurt dressing over the salads.

Makes 4 servings

Crescent Rolls

Purchase refrigerated crescent roll dough and bake as directed.

Lemon-Raspberry Pudding Cake

^{2}/$_3$ **cup sugar**

^{1}/$_4$ **cup flour**

1 **tablespoon grated lemon zest**

^{1}/$_8$ **teaspoon salt**

1 **cup buttermilk**

3 **egg yolks**

^{1}/$_4$ **cup fresh lemon juice**

2 **tablespoons butter, melted**

3 **egg whites, at room temperature**

1 **(12-ounce) package frozen raspberries, thawed and drained**

Boiling water

Preheat the oven to 350°F. Butter an 8-inch round or 8x8x2-inch baking dish.

Combine the sugar, flour, lemon zest, and salt in a large bowl. Whisk the buttermilk, egg yolks, lemon juice, and butter in a medium bowl until well blended. Pour the buttermilk mixture into the flour mixture; whisk until smooth.

Beat the egg whites in a large bowl with an electric mixer at high speed until soft peaks form; fold into the batter. Gently fold in the raspberries. Pour into the prepared baking dish. Place the dish in a roasting pan. Pull out the oven rack and place the roasting pan on the rack. Pour enough boiling water into the pan to come one-third up the side of the baking dish.

Bake for 35 minutes or until the surface springs back when lightly touched in the center. Cool for 10 minutes on a wire rack. Serve warm. Refrigerate any leftover cake.

Makes 6 servings

Smoked Salmon Salad

Flavorful smoked salmon drizzled with a mango dressing is a delightful taste sensation.

1 pound fresh asparagus, trimmed

2 mangoes, peeled, pitted, and diced

2/3 cup plain yogurt

2 tablespoons chopped fresh chives

1 tablespoon white wine vinegar

1 tablespoon sugar

1 head Boston lettuce, torn

2 ripe tomatoes, sliced

3 cups chopped smoked salmon

Cook the asparagus in a large pot of boiling water for 2 to 3 minutes or until crisp-tender. Drain and rinse under cold water; refrigerate for at least 30 minutes before serving.

Place the diced mango in the bowl of a food processor; pulse for 1 minute or until fruit is smooth. Add the yogurt, chives, vinegar, and sugar; pulse for 30 seconds or until combined. Refrigerate until ready to serve.

Arrange the lettuce leaves on 4 dinner plates. Place the asparagus and tomato slices around the outside of each plate; arrange the salmon in the middle. Drizzle the dressing over the salads.

Makes 4 servings

TIP

Smoked salmon can be found in the refrigerated seafood section of your local supermarket. Canned skinless, boneless pink salmon can be substituted.

Smoked Salmon Salad

Red Pepper Crostini

Oatmeal Toffee Cookies

Red Pepper Crostini

1/4 cup butter, melted

1 teaspoon minced garlic

16 slices Italian bread, sliced 1/2- to 3/4-inch thick

2/3 cup freshly shredded Parmesan cheese

1 (12-ounce) jar roasted red peppers, cut into strips

8 slices Provolone cheese, cut in half

Preheat the broiler.

Combine butter and garlic in a small bowl; set aside. Place bread on an ungreased 15x10x1-inch baking sheet. Broil 6 inches from heat for 2 to 4 minutes or until bread is lightly toasted. Turn toasted side over; brush top with melted butter mixture. Sprinkle each slice with Parmesan cheese; top with red pepper and 1/2 slice Provolone cheese. Return to broiler; broil for 2 to 3 minutes or until cheese is melted and starting to brown. Serve warm.

Makes 16 pieces

Oatmeal Toffee Cookies

1 1/2 cups flour

1 teaspoon baking soda

1/2 teaspoon baking powder

1/4 teaspoon salt

3/4 cup (1 1/2 sticks) butter, softened

1/2 cup packed brown sugar

1/2 cup granulated sugar

2 eggs

1 teaspoon vanilla extract

3 cups old-fashioned oats

2 cups English toffee-flavored bits

3/4 cup chopped pecans

Preheat the oven to 350°F. Grease 2 cookie sheets.

Sift together the flour, baking soda, baking powder, and salt; set aside. Beat the butter and sugars in a large bowl with an electric mixer at high speed until fluffy. Add the eggs and vanilla; beat until combined. Gradually add the flour mixture, beating at low speed until combined. Stir in the oats, toffee bits, and pecans by hand with a wooden spoon

Drop the dough by rounded teaspoonfuls 2 inches apart onto the prepared cookie sheets. Bake for 10 to 12 minutes or until browned. Cool on the pans for 10 minutes. Remove to wire racks; cool completely.

Makes 4 dozen cookies

Creamy Shrimp Salad

Shrimp tossed with a creamy dressing and accompanied with fresh asparagus makes a delightful summer lunch or dinner.

$^1/_3$ **cup mayonnaise**

2 **tablespoons ketchup**

1 **teaspoon fresh lemon juice**

$^1/_2$ **teaspoon Worcestershire sauce**

2 **tablespoons minced red pepper**

2 **tablespoons pickle relish**

2 **teaspoons dried dill**

1 **pound cooked medium shrimp, peeled, deveined, and cut into halves**

$^1/_2$ **cup diced celery**

1 **pound fresh asparagus, trimmed**

Boston or Bibb lettuce leaves

2 **mangoes, peeled, pitted and sliced**

Whisk together the mayonnaise, ketchup, lemon juice, and Worcestershire sauce in a large bowl. Add the red pepper, pickle relish, and dill; stir to combine. Add the shrimp and celery; toss to coat. Refrigerate for at least 1 hour before serving.

Cook the asparagus in a large pot of boiling water for 2 to 3 minutes or until crisp-tender. Drain and rinse under cold water; refrigerate for at least 30 minutes before serving.

Arrange the lettuce leaves on 4 dinner plates; top with the asparagus spears and the shrimp salad. Arrange mango slices around the outside of each plate.

Makes 4 servings

Banana Bread

1³/₄ **cups flour**

1 **teaspoon baking soda**

¹/₂ **teaspoon baking powder**

¹/₈ **teaspoon salt**

¹/₂ **cup (1 stick) butter, softened**

1 **cup sugar**

1 **teaspoon vanilla extract**

2 **eggs**

¹/₄ **cup milk**

3 **medium ripe bananas, peeled and mashed**

Preheat the oven to 350°F. Spray an 8x4x2-inch loaf pan with cooking spray.

Sift together the flour, baking soda, baking powder, and salt; set aside. Beat the butter, sugar, and vanilla in a large bowl with an electric mixer at high speed until fluffy. Add the eggs, milk, and mashed bananas; mix to combine. Add the flour mixture; beat until combined. Pour the batter into the prepared loaf pan. Bake for 45 to 55 minutes or until a wooden pick inserted into the center comes out clean. Cool in the pan for 10 minutes. Run a small knife between the bread and the sides of the pan. Remove from the pan to a wire rack; cool completely.

Makes 1 loaf

Blueberry-Raspberry Tart

Crust

2 **cups vanilla wafer crumbs**

6 **tablespoons butter, melted**

Filling

1 **(8-ounce) package cream cheese, softened**

¹/₂ **cup sugar**

1 **(6-ounce) container raspberry yogurt**

3 **cups fresh blueberries**

Spray a 9-inch tart pan with a removable bottom with cooking spray.

To make the crust: Combine the vanilla wafer crumbs and butter in a large bowl. Toss with a fork until the crumbs are moistened. Press onto the bottom and side of the prepared pan; set aside.

To make the filling: Beat the cream cheese and sugar in a medium bowl with an electric mixer at high speed until smooth. Add the yogurt and beat at low speed until well blended. Pour into the crust, spreading evenly. Refrigerate, loosely covered, for 4 hours or until set.

To serve, gently loosen and remove the edge of the pan. Top with the blueberries.

Makes 8 servings

Jamaican Shrimp Salad

Sweet, sour, and spicy create a delicious blend of flavors in this grilled shrimp salad.

1 cup unsweetened pineapple juice

1 teaspoon grated lime zest

3 tablespoons fresh lime juice

1 tablespoon vegetable oil

1 to 2 teaspoons minced garlic, to taste

$1/2$ teaspoon dried thyme

$1/2$ teaspoon dried oregano

$1/4$ teaspoon cinnamon

$1/4$ teaspoon ground allspice

2 tablespoons Jamaican jerk sauce

20 jumbo shrimp (about 1 pound), peeled and deveined

3 cups cooked white rice

1 (15-ounce) can black beans, rinsed and drained

Salt and pepper, to taste

2 cups fresh pineapple chunks

6 green onions, trimmed and cut into 2-inch lengths

1 head Boston lettuce, torn

Lime slices, as a garnish

Bring the pineapple juice to a boil in a small saucepan over medium-high heat; cook for 8 to 10 minutes or until reduced to $1/3$ cup. Remove from heat and whisk in the lime zest, lime juice, oil, garlic, thyme, oregano, cinnamon, and allspice. Let the marinade cool to room temperature.

In a resealable plastic bag, combine the jerk sauce and $1/4$ cup of the pineapple juice marinade. Add the shrimp and toss to coat; refrigerate for 30 minutes.

Mix the rice and black beans with the remaining marinade in a large bowl. Season with salt and pepper; set aside.

Prepare a medium-hot fire in a charcoal or gas grill; oil the grill grate with cooking spray. Remove the shrimp from the marinade; add the pineapple chunks and onions to the marinade, turning to coat. Thread 4 long or 8 short skewers with the shrimp, pineapple, and onions; brush with the marinade. Grill the skewers, turning once, for 6 to 8 minutes, until the shrimp turn pink. Divide the lettuce among 4 dinner plates; spoon the rice mixture on top. Remove the shrimp, pineapple, and onions from the skewers; arrange on top of the rice. Serve garnished with lime slices.

Makes 4 servings

TIPS

Prepared jerk sauce can be found in the condiment section of most supermarkets.

Use any remaining fresh pineapple to make Pineapple Crisp for dessert.

Pineapple-Macadamia Muffins

2 cups flour

1/3 cup packed brown sugar

2 teaspoons baking powder

1/4 teaspoon salt

1 cup chopped macadamia nuts

2/3 cup flaked coconut

2/3 cup milk

1 (8-ounce) can crushed
   pineapple, undrained

1/2 cup butter, melted

1 egg, lightly beaten

1 teaspoon vanilla extract

Preheat the oven to 350°F. Spray muffin cups with cooking spray.

Combine the flour, brown sugar, baking powder, and salt in a large bowl. Stir in the macadamia nuts and coconut; set aside. Stir the milk, pineapple, butter, egg, and vanilla together in a small bowl. Add the egg mixture to the flour mixture; stir by hand until combined. Spoon the batter into the prepared muffin cups. Bake for 20 to 22 minutes or until a wooden pick inserted into the center comes out clean. Cool in the pan on a wire rack for 5 minutes. Remove the muffins from the pan. Serve warm.

Makes 12 muffins

Pineapple Crisp

Topping

1/4 cup flour, sifted

1/4 cup packed brown sugar

1/2 teaspoon cinnamon

1/8 teaspoon ground nutmeg

3 tablespoons butter, cold and
   cut into small pieces

1/4 cup granola

1/4 cup chopped macadamia nuts

1/4 cup flaked coconut

Filling

2 cups chopped fresh pineapple

2 tablespoons sugar

1 tablespoon dark rum

Preheat the oven to 375°F. Spray four 8-ounce ramekins with cooking spray.

To make the topping: Combine the flour, brown sugar, cinnamon, and nutmeg in a medium bowl. Cut in the butter with a pastry blender or 2 knives until the mixture resembles coarse crumbs. Stir in the granola, macadamia nuts, and coconut; set aside.

To make the filling: Combine the pineapple, sugar, and rum in a medium bowl. Spoon the mixture into the prepared ramekins. Sprinkle the topping evenly over the fruit, lightly pressing it in place. Bake for 20 to 25 minutes or until the filling is bubbling. Serve warm or at room temperature.

Makes 4 servings

Seafood Pasta Salad

*This elegant seafood salad is a great dish to serve
for a dinner party and it can be prepared ahead of time.*

3 cups uncooked fusilli

1 pound bay scallops, rinsed

1 cup dry white wine

1 pound cooked medium
shrimp, peeled and deveined

2 cups frozen peas, thawed

$^1/_2$ cup chopped red pepper

$^1/_3$ cup diced red onion

2 cups packed fresh basil leaves

3 garlic cloves, crushed

2 tablespoons plus 1 cup extra-
virgin olive oil

5 tablespoons fresh lemon juice

Salt and freshly ground black
pepper, to taste

$^1/_2$ cup sliced ripe olives

$^1/_2$ cup toasted pine nuts

$^1/_2$ cup freshly shredded
Parmesan cheese

Prepare the fusilli according to package directions; drain.
Cook the scallops in wine in a large skillet over medium heat
for 5 minutes or until opaque; drain. Combine the fusilli,
scallops, shrimp, peas, red pepper and onion in a large bowl;
set aside.

Combine the basil, garlic, and 2 tablespoons oil in a food
processor; process until a paste forms. Add 1 cup oil, lemon
juice, salt, and pepper; process until well blended. Pour the
dressing over the fusilli mixture; toss to coat. Refrigerate
for at least 1 hour before serving.

Just before serving, sprinkle the salad with the olives, pine
nuts, and Parmesan cheese; toss to combine.

Makes 6 to 8 servings

TIP

Some of the dressing will be absorbed if the salad is refrigerated overnight. In that case, simply add enough olive oil to
moisten the salad.

Foccacia Bread

Purchase foccacia bread to warm in the oven or serve another easy-to-prepare bread. Or, make the Tomato Bread on page 67.

Almond Biscotti

¹/₂ **cup almond paste**

3 **eggs**

³/₄ **cup sugar**

2 **teaspoons grated lemon zest**

¹/₂ **teaspoon almond extract**

1 ²/₃ **cups flour**

¹/₃ **cup cornstarch**

¹/₂ **teaspoon baking powder**

¹/₄ **teaspoon salt**

³/₄ **cup coarsely chopped almonds**

Spray a 15x10x1-inch baking sheet with cooking spray.

Place the almond paste and eggs in a food processor. Cover and process on high speed about 20 seconds or until smooth. Add the sugar, lemon zest, and almond extract; process until combined.

Sift the flour, cornstarch, baking powder and salt in a large bowl. Add the almond mixture; stir with a wooden spoon to combine. Using flour-coated hands, finish mixing the dough by hand until the flour is completely incorporated. Fold in the nuts. Divide the dough into halves. Shape each half into a 9x3-inch log on the prepared baking sheet. Refrigerate for at least 1 hour.

Preheat the oven to 350°F. Bake for 18 to 20 minutes or until a wooden pick inserted into the centers comes out clean. Cool on the pan for 15 minutes. *Reduce the oven temperature to 325°F.*

With a serrated knife, cut each log diagonally into ¹/₂-inch-thick slices. Place the slices, cut sides down, on the same baking sheet. Bake at 325°F for 8 to 10 minutes. Turn the slices over; bake for 8 to10 minutes, until dry and crisp. Cool completely on a wire rack. Store in an airtight container at room temperature for up to 2 days or freeze for up to 6 months.

Makes 2 dozen cookies

Shrimp and Avocado Salad

A cilantro-lime dressing accents shrimp, rice, and black beans in this southwestern-style salad.

1 pound cooked, peeled shrimp, cooled to room temperature

2 cups cooked white rice, cooled to room temperature

1 (15-ounce) can black beans, rinsed and drained

1 red pepper, diced

1 cup seeded, diced cucumber

¼ cup minced green onion

3 tablespoons fresh lime juice

1 tablespoon white wine vinegar

1 garlic clove, minced

¼ cup chopped fresh cilantro

3 tablespoons extra-virgin olive oil

½ teaspoon salt

⅛ teaspoon black pepper

   Boston lettuce leaves

1 avocado, peeled, pitted and diced

Combine the shrimp, rice, beans, red pepper, cucumber, and green onion in a large bowl; set aside. Combine the lime juice, vinegar, garlic, and cilantro in a small bowl. Whisk in the oil, salt, and black pepper. Pour the dressing over the shrimp mixture; toss to coat. Arrange the lettuce leaves on 4 dinner plates; top with the shrimp salad and sprinkle with the diced avocado.

Makes 4 servings

TIPS

Select avocados that yield to gentle pressure and store them in the refrigerator. If an avocado is firm, ripen at room temperature for several days or, more quickly, in a closed paper bag.

To pit an avocado, do not remove the skin. Cut the avocado in half down to the pit. Twist the halves to separate. Holding the half with the pit in one hand, carefully strike the pit with the blade of a sturdy knife to wedge the blade firmly into the pit. Twist and lift the knife to remove the pit.

To scoop out and slice or dice an avocado, slide a large spoon between the avocado flesh and the skin. Scoop out the flesh in one piece. Place it, cut side down, on a work surface. Slice with a small knife. Cut across the slices to dice the avocado to the desired size.

Sweet Corn Muffins

1 1/4 **cups flour**

3/4 **cup yellow cornmeal**

1/2 **teaspoon salt**

1 **tablespoon baking powder**

1/3 **cup sugar**

1 **egg, beaten**

1 **cup milk**

1/4 **cup vegetable oil**

Preheat the oven to 400°F. Spray muffin cups with cooking spray.

Combine the flour, cornmeal, salt, baking powder, and sugar in a large bowl; set aside.

Stir together the egg, milk, and oil in a small bowl. Add the egg mixture to the flour mixture; stir by hand until combined. Spoon the batter into the prepared muffin cups. Bake for 20 to 22 minutes or until a wooden pick inserted into the center comes out clean. Cool in the pan on a wire rack for 5 minutes. Remove the muffins from the pan. Serve warm.

Makes 12 muffins

Peach and Blueberry Ambrosia

3 **tablespoons honey**

1 1/2 **tablespoons fresh lemon juice**

1 **teaspoon grated lemon zest**

2 **peaches, peeled, pitted, and diced**

2 **cups fresh blueberries**

1 **cup chilled sparkling wine**

Heat the honey and lemon juice in a small saucepan over low heat until the honey melts. Remove from the heat; stir in the lemon zest. Cool for 10 minutes.

Combine the peaches, blueberries, and honey syrup in a small bowl, stirring gently. Spoon into 4 tall sundae dishes or wine glasses. Refrigerate for 2 hours. To serve, pour 1/4 cup sparkling wine into each dish.

Makes 4 servings

Shrimp Couscous Salad

Make this easy and quick shrimp salad for a picnic or a casual summer supper at home.

2 tablespoons fresh lemon juice

¹/₄ cup extra-virgin olive oil

¹/₂ teaspoon ground cumin

2 cups vegetable broth

1 tablespoon butter

1 (10-ounce) package plain couscous

1 pound cooked medium shrimp, peeled and deveined

1 (11-ounce) can mandarin oranges, drained and cut into halves

1 cup chopped cherry tomatoes, seeds removed

¹/₂ cup golden raisins

¹/₂ cup sliced almonds

¹/₄ cup minced green onions

Whisk together the lemon juice, olive oil and cumin in a small bowl; set aside.

Bring the vegetable broth and butter to a boil in a medium saucepan. Stir in the couscous; cover. Remove from heat; let stand for 5 to 10 minutes or until broth is absorbed. Transfer the couscous to a large bowl; fluff with a fork. Cool to room temperature.

Add the shrimp, oranges, tomatoes, raisins, almonds, and green onions to the cooled couscous; gently mix together. Pour the dressing over the salad; toss to coat.

Makes 6 servings

TIP

Although it looks like a grain, couscous is actually a form of pasta made from steaming and drying cracked durum wheat. Couscous is widely available in the quick-cooking variety that only needs to be soaked in hot water.

Tomato Cornmeal Tart

Dough

- 3 tablespoons sour cream
- 1/3 cup cold water
- 1 cup flour
- 1/4 cup yellow cornmeal
- 1 teaspoon sugar
- 1/2 teaspoon salt
- 6 tablespoons butter, cold and cut into small pieces

Topping

- 1 cup shredded mozzarella cheese
- 3 tablespoons chopped fresh basil
- 2 large ripe tomatoes, cut into 1/4-inch-thick slices
- 1/2 teaspoon sugar
- 1/8 teaspoon salt
- 1/8 teaspoon pepper
- 1 egg, beaten

To make the crust: Stir the sour cream and cold water together in a small bowl; set aside. Process the flour, cornmeal, sugar, and salt in a food processor until blended. Add the butter. Pulse until the mixture resembles coarse crumbs. Add the sour cream mixture; pulse just until moist clumps form. Do not overprocess. Gather the dough into a ball; flatten into a disk. Wrap in plastic wrap; refrigerate for at least 1 hour.

Preheat the oven to 400°F.

Roll out the dough to an 11-inch circle between 2 sheets of parchment paper. Remove top sheet of parchment paper; slide the crust onto a baking sheet, keeping bottom parchment in place.

To make the topping: Toss the cheese and basil together in a bowl. Sprinkle the cheese mixture over the dough, spreading to within 3 inches of the edge. Arrange the tomato slices over the cheese; sprinkle with the sugar, salt, and pepper. Fold the outer edge of the dough over the tomatoes, using the parchment paper as an aid. Overlap the dough slightly while folding and press gently to seal. (The dough will only partially cover the tomatoes.) Brush the crust with the egg.

Bake for 30 minutes or until the pastry is golden brown. Cool on a wire rack for 10 minutes. Serve warm or at room temperature. Cut into 8 wedges.

Makes 8 pieces

Shrimp and Watermelon Salad

Refreshing fruit—watermelon and pineapple—accompany spicy grilled jumbo shrimp in this tropical salad.

2 tablespoons Mexican seasoning

1 teaspoon cinnamon

1 dozen jumbo shrimp, peeled, deveined, and tails removed

2 cups cubed, seeded watermelon

1 (20-ounce) can pineapple chunks, drained

¼ cup diced green pepper

1 teaspoon finely chopped, seeded jalapeño pepper (optional)

½ cup diced, peeled cucumber

2 tablespoons fresh lime juice

2 tablespoons soy sauce

2 tablespoons honey

1 tablespoon olive oil

8 cups torn romaine lettuce

2 tablespoons chopped fresh cilantro

Mix the Mexican seasoning and cinnamon in a small bowl. Dredge the shrimp in the seasonings; set aside. Combine the watermelon, pineapple, peppers, and cucumber in a medium bowl; cover and refrigerate. Whisk together the lime juice, soy sauce, honey, and oil; set aside.

Prepare a medium-hot fire in a charcoal or gas grill; oil the grill grate with cooking spray. Thread the shrimp onto 4 long or 8 short skewers. Grill the skewers, turning once, for 5 to 6 minutes, until the shrimp are opaque.

Divide the lettuce among 4 dinner plates; top with the shrimp and the fruit mixture. Drizzle the dressing over the salads; sprinkle with chopped cilantro.

Makes 4 servings

TIP

You can find Mexican seasoning in the spice section of your local supermarket. It is a blend of cumin, chili peppers, onion, and garlic.

Cucumber Rounds

$^1/_3$ **cup spreadable cheese**

16 **slices cocktail rye bread**

16 **($^1/_4$-inch-thick) slices unpeeled cucumber**

Spread each slice of bread with 1 teaspoon cheese. Top with a cucumber slice.

TIP

You can find a selection of spreadable cheese flavors in the refrigerated specialty cheese section of your local supermarket. Camembert or any other soft cheese also can be used.

Caramelized Bananas and Ice Cream

3 **teaspoons granulated sugar**

3 **teaspoons cinnamon**

6 **tablespoons butter**

2 **cups packed brown sugar**

4 **large ripe bananas, peeled**

8 **scoops vanilla ice cream**

Combine the granulated sugar and cinnamon in small bowl; set aside. Melt the butter and brown sugar in a large skillet over medium heat; cook until bubbling. Cut the bananas crosswise into halves, then cut each half lengthwise, forming 4 pieces per banana. Place the bananas, cut sides down, in the pan; spoon the caramelized sugar mixture over the bananas. Cook for 2 minutes.

Remove the pan from the heat. For each serving, place 2 scoops ice cream into a dessert bowl. Top with 4 banana pieces and a spoonful of sauce. Serve immediately.

Makes 4 servings

Shrimp and Vegetable Salad

Tossing fresh vegetables and shrimp with a picánte sauce dressing makes a scrumptious meal.

½ **pound fresh green beans, trimmed**

2 **cups chopped ripe tomato**

1 **cup thinly sliced red onion, separated into rings**

1 **pound cooked medium shrimp, peeled and deveined**

12 **medium pitted ripe olives, cut into halves**

2 **cups whole kernel corn**

1½ **cups picánte sauce**

2 **tablespoons white wine vinegar**

2 **tablespoons olive oil**

1½ **teaspoons minced fresh tarragon or ½ teaspoon dried tarragon**

9 **cups mixed greens**

Place the green beans in the steamer basket of a medium saucepan over 1 inch of water; bring to a boil. Cover and steam for 5 minutes or until crisp-tender; drain and set aside to cool.

Combine the cooled beans, tomato, onion, shrimp, olives, and corn in a large bowl; toss well and set aside. Whisk together the picánte sauce, vinegar, oil, and tarragon in a small bowl. Pour the dressing over the shrimp mixture; toss to coat. Refrigerate until ready to serve. Divide the greens among 6 dinner plates; top with the shrimp salad mixture.

Makes 6 servings

TIP

You can use fresh, canned, or thawed frozen corn in this recipe.

Peach Cobbler

Topping

- ³/₄ **cup flour**
- ¹/₃ **cup sugar**
- ¹/₄ **cup cornmeal**
- 1¹/₂ **teaspoons baking powder**
- ¹/₈ **teaspoon salt**
- 3 **tablespoons butter, cold and cut into small pieces**
- ¹/₃ **cup milk**

Filling

- 3 **pounds peaches, peeled, pitted and cut into ¹/₂-inch slices**
- 2 **tablespoons fresh lemon juice**
- ¹/₂ **teaspoon vanilla extract**
- 3 **tablespoons sugar**
- 2 **teaspoons cornstarch**
- ¹/₄ **teaspoon cinnamon**

Whipped cream, as a garnish

Preheat the oven to 375°F. Spray a 9x9x2-inch baking dish with cooking spray.

To make the topping: Whisk together the flour, sugar, cornmeal, baking powder, and salt in a medium bowl. Cut in the butter with a pastry blender or 2 knives until the mixture resembles coarse crumbs. Stir in the milk just until a stiff dough forms; set aside.

To make the filling: Combine the peaches, lemon juice, and vanilla in a large bowl; set aside. Combine the sugar, cornstarch, and cinnamon in a small bowl. Add the sugar mixture to the peaches and stir gently to combine. Spoon evenly into the prepared baking dish.

Drop the topping by heaping tablespoonfuls onto the filling, spacing evenly. Bake for about 45 minutes or until the filling is bubbling and a wooden pick inserted into the topping comes out clean. Serve warm garnished with whipped cream.

Makes 8 servings

Strawberry Shrimp Salad

*Shrimp topped with a strawberry vinaigrette dressing
makes a delightful luncheon or dinner.*

1 cup chopped fresh strawberries

2 tablespoons red wine vinegar

3 teaspoons chopped fresh basil
or 1 teaspoon dried basil

1/2 teaspoon sugar

Dash pepper

1 cup fresh pea pods

1 pound fresh large shrimp,
shelled and deveined or
1 pound frozen shelled and
deveined large shrimp, thawed

1/2 teaspoon lemon-pepper
seasoning

2 cups torn spinach leaves

2 cups torn red leaf lettuce

1 cup sliced fresh mushrooms

1 (11-ounce) can mandarin
oranges, drained

1/4 cup walnuts, toasted

1/3 cup crumbled blue cheese

Whole strawberries,
as a garnish (optional)

Place the chopped strawberries, vinegar, basil, sugar, and pepper in an electric blender or food processor. Cover and blend or process on high speed about 20 seconds or until smooth; set aside.

Cook the pea pods in 2 cups boiling water in a medium saucepan for 2 to 3 minutes or until crisp-tender; drain and set aside to cool.

Sprinkle the shrimp with the lemon-pepper seasoning. Sauté the shrimp in a large skillet coated with cooking spray for 3 to 4 minutes, turning frequently, until shrimp turn pink.

Toss the spinach, lettuce, mushrooms, oranges, and pea pods in a large bowl. Divide the spinach mixture among 4 dinner plates; top with the shrimp. Drizzle the dressing over the salad and sprinkle with walnuts and blue cheese. Garnish with strawberries, if desired.

Makes 4 servings

Whole Wheat Rolls

Purchase whole wheat rolls to warm in the oven or serve another easy-to-prepare bread. Or, make the Honey Whole Wheat Dinner Rolls on page 3.

Strawberry Shortbread Tarts

2/3 **cup flour**

  2 **tablespoons cornstarch**

1/4 **teaspoon baking powder**

1/4 **teaspoon salt**

10 **tablespoons butter, softened**

1/3 **cup confectioners' sugar**

  1 **teaspoon vanilla extract**

1/2 **cup (4 ounces) cream cheese, softened**

3/4 **cup prepared lemon curd, chilled**

  1 **pint fresh strawberries, sliced**

Sift together the flour, cornstarch, baking powder, and salt; set aside. Beat the butter, confectioners' sugar, and vanilla in a large bowl with an electric mixer at high speed until fluffy. Add the flour mixture. Beat at low speed just until moist clumps form. Gather the dough into a ball; flatten into a disk. Wrap in plastic wrap; refrigerate for at least 1 hour.

Preheat the oven to 325°F. Grease a large cookie sheet.

Roll out the dough 1/4 inch thick on a lightly floured surface. Cut out with a 3-inch round cookie cutter. Reroll and cut the dough scraps to make a total of 8 cookies. Place 2 inches apart on the prepared pan. Bake for about 15 minutes or until lightly browned at the edges. Cool completely on the pan on a wire rack.

Beat the cream cheese in a medium bowl with an electric mixer at high speed until smooth. Stir the lemon curd until smooth; fold into the cream cheese. Place the cookies on serving plates. Spread the lemon mixture evenly over the cookies. Arrange the strawberries on top.

Makes 8 cookies

TIP

Lemon curd is usually found on the shelf with the jam and jelly at your local supermarket.

Tropical Shrimp Salad

Fresh lime juice, coconut milk, and chutney bring a taste of the tropics to this luscious shrimp salad meal—especially when topped off with Cherry Pecan Bars for dessert.

8 ounces uncooked angel hair pasta

1 teaspoon sesame oil

1 pound cooked medium shrimp, peeled and deveined

1/2 cup fresh lime juice

1/2 teaspoon salt

2 cucumbers, peeled, seeded, and chopped

4 green onions, sliced

1 red pepper, cut into thin strips

1 cup chopped roasted cashews

1/2 cup coconut milk

1/3 cup mango chutney

1/4 to 1/2 teaspoon crushed red pepper flakes

1/4 cup chopped fresh cilantro

Prepare the pasta according to package directions; drain. Toss the pasta with the sesame oil and refrigerate until ready to serve.

Toss the shrimp with the lime juice and salt in a resealable plastic bag; refrigerate for 30 minutes. Combine the cucumbers, onions, pepper, and cashews in a large bowl; set aside. Mix the coconut milk and chutney in a small bowl; pour over the cucumber mixture. Add the shrimp and marinade, red pepper flakes, and cilantro; toss to coat. Divide the pasta among 4 dinner plates; top with the shrimp mixture.

Makes 4 servings

TIP

Mango chutney—mangoes mixed with red chili pepper, lime, and spices—can be found in the condiment section or the Asian section of your local supermarket.

Italian or French Bread

Purchase Italian mini loaves or French baguettes to warm in the oven. Serve with homemade honey butter—simply mix a little honey with softened butter!

Cherry Pecan Bars

Crust

1 3/4 **cups flour**

2/3 **cup confectioners' sugar**

1/4 **cup cornstarch**

1/2 **teaspoon salt**

3/4 **cup (1 1/2 sticks) butter, cold and cut into small pieces**

Topping

1/4 **cup (1/2 stick) butter**

1 1/4 **cups packed light brown sugar**

1/2 **cup light corn syrup**

4 **cups pecans, coarsely chopped**

2 **cups dried cherries**

3/4 **cup heavy cream**

2 **teaspoons vanilla extract**

Preheat the oven to 350°F. Line a 13x9x2-inch baking pan with foil, leaving a 1-inch overhang on all sides. Butter the foil.

To make the crust: Process the flour, confectioners' sugar, cornstarch, and salt in a food processor until blended. Add the butter. Pulse until moist clumps form. Press onto the bottom of the prepared pan. Bake for 25 to 30 minutes or until lightly browned. Cool completely on a wire rack. *Reduce the oven temperature to 325°F.*

To make the topping: Melt the butter in a large saucepan over low heat. Add the brown sugar and corn syrup. Cook over medium heat, stirring constantly, until the sugar dissolves and the mixture comes to a boil. Boil for 1 minute. Stir in the pecans, dried cherries, and cream. Return to a boil. Cook for 3 minutes, stirring constantly, until the mixture thickens. Remove from the heat. Stir in the vanilla. Spread the topping evenly over the crust. Bake at 325°F for 20 to 25 minutes or until the topping darkens and is bubbling. Cool completely in the pan on a wire rack. Using the foil, lift from the pan to a cutting board. Cut into 2x1-inch bars with a sharp knife.

Makes 4 dozen bars

TIP

Store bars layered between sheets of waxed paper in an airtight container at room temperature.

Grilled Tuna with Orange & Jicama

*Crispy jicama and sweet oranges tossed with a caramelized
onion dressing complement grilled tuna steaks in this recipe.*

4 teaspoons olive oil

1 large onion, cut into thin slices

2 teaspoons sugar

1/4 cup red wine vinegar

1/2 cup fresh orange juice

1/4 cup extra-virgin olive oil

2 teaspoons ground cumin

1/8 teaspoon salt

1/8 teaspoon black pepper

1/2 cup fresh orange juice

4 ahi tuna steaks (6 ounces each)

2 navel oranges

2 cups diced, peeled jicama

1 red pepper, diced

8 cups torn red leaf lettuce

Heat 4 teaspoons olive oil in a large skillet. Break the onion
rings apart; place in skillet. Sprinkle with the sugar. Cook,
stirring occasionally, for 15 minutes or until tender and
browned. Remove from heat and let cool to room temperature.
Place the onions into a blender or food processor. Add vinegar,
1/2 cup orange juice, 1/4 cup extra-virgin olive oil, cumin, salt,
and black pepper to the blender; puree until smooth. Set
aside. *(Dressing can be made up to 8 hours in advance and
stored in the refrigerator. Bring to room temperature before
serving.)*

Pour 1/2 cup orange juice into a resealable plastic bag. Add
the tuna and turn to coat; refrigerate for 30 minutes.

Cut off and discard both ends of the oranges. Stand each one
upright on a cutting board. Cut downward in vertical strips
following the curve of the orange to remove the peel and
pith. Working over a large bowl to catch the juice, cut down
on either side of each membrane to release and lift out the
individual orange sections. Squeeze the juice from the
membranes into the bowl over the orange sections. Add
the jicama, red pepper, and reserved onions to the orange
sections. Toss to combine.

Prepare a medium-hot fire in a charcoal or gas grill; oil the
grill grate with cooking spray. Grill the tuna for 4 to 5 minutes
a side or until fish reaches desired degree of doneness (medium-rare is very pink in the center; medium is light pink in
the center; well-done is evenly colored throughout).

Add the lettuce to the vegetables. Pour the reserved dressing
over the salad; toss to coat.

Divide the salad among 4 dinner plates; top with the tuna.

Makes 4 servings

Crusty Wheat Bread

Purchase crusty wheat bread or rolls to warm in the oven.

Orange Cheesecake Bars

Crust

2 **cups vanilla wafer crumbs**

¹/₃ **cup butter, melted**

2 **tablespoons sugar**

Filling

2 **(8-ounce) packages cream cheese, softened**

³/₄ **cup sugar**

2 **eggs**

¹/₂ **cup sour cream**

1 **teaspoon vanilla extract**

Topping

4 **ounces white baking chocolate, chopped**

¹/₂ **cup heavy cream**

2 **tablespoons butter**

¹/₃ **cup frozen orange juice concentrate, thawed**

2 **teaspoons grated orange zest**

Preheat the oven to 350°F. Spray a 13x9x2-inch baking pan with cooking spray.

To make the crust: Combine the vanilla wafer crumbs, butter, and sugar in a small bowl. Toss with a fork until the crumbs are moistened. Press onto the bottom of the prepared pan. Bake for 15 minutes. Cool completely on a wire rack.

To make the filling: Beat the cream cheese and sugar in a large bowl with an electric mixer at high speed until blended. Add the eggs, one at a time, beating well after each addition. Add the sour cream and vanilla; beat at medium speed until combined. Spread evenly over the crust. Bake for 30 to 35 minutes or until set. Cool completely in the pan on a wire rack.

To make the topping: Place the white chocolate in a large bowl. Bring the cream and butter to a simmer in a small saucepan over medium-high heat. Pour the cream mixture over the white chocolate. Whisk until the chocolate is melted and smooth. Add the orange juice concentrate and orange zest; stir until combined. Refrigerate for about 45 minutes, stirring occasionally, until slightly thickened but still spreadable. Spread the topping evenly over the bars. Refrigerate, covered, for at least 1 hour before serving. Cut into 36 squares.

Makes 3 dozen bars

Niçoise Salad

*This classic French salad can be prepared easily in advance.
Grill the tuna steaks or use canned tuna.*

1 pound small red potatoes,
cut into ¹/₂-inch cubes

1 pound green beans, trimmed

4 ahi tuna steaks (6 ounces each)

3 tablespoons fresh lemon juice

1 teaspoon freshly ground pepper

2 tablespoons red wine vinegar

1 tablespoon fresh lemon juice

1 teaspoon Dijon mustard

1 teaspoon minced garlic

¹/₄ teaspoon pepper

¹/₈ teaspoon salt

¹/₂ cup extra-virgin olive oil

2 heads Boston lettuce, torn

4 hard-cooked eggs, peeled and
halved lengthwise

2 cups cherry tomatoes, halved

³/₄ cup Niçoise olives or ³/₄ cup
Kalamata olives

Place potatoes in a medium-sized saucepan and cover with water by 1 inch. Bring to a boil over medium heat and cook for 15 minutes or until tender; drain. Set aside to cool. Place the green beans in a steamer basket. Place the basket in a saucepan over 1 inch of water; bring to a boil. Cover and steam for 5 minutes or until crisp-tender; drain. Set aside to cool.

Place the tuna on a serving platter; drizzle with 3 tablespoons lemon juice and sprinkle with 1 teaspoon freshly ground pepper. Marinate the tuna in the refrigerator for at least 15 minutes. Prepare a medium-hot fire in a charcoal or gas grill; oil the grill grate with cooking spray. Grill the tuna steaks for 3 to 6 minutes a side over medium-high heat or until fish reaches desired degree of doneness (medium-rare is very pink in the center; medium is light pink in the center; well-done is evenly colored throughout). Set aside to cool; cut tuna into bite-size pieces.

Combine the vinegar, 1 tablespoon lemon juice, mustard, garlic, ¹/₄ teaspoon pepper, and salt in a small bowl. Whisk in the oil; set aside.

Place the lettuce on a large serving platter. Arrange the eggs, potatoes, green beans, tomatoes, olives, and tuna on top of the lettuce. Drizzle the dressing over the salad.

Makes 6 servings

TIPS

Three (6-ounce) cans of water-packed tuna can be substituted for fresh.

Niçoise olives—after which this recipe is named—are small, purplish-black in color, and have a distinctive sour flavor. They can be purchased at specialty grocery stores and in some supermarkets. Kalamata olives are a good substitute.

Goat Cheese Toasts

1 **French baguette, cut into ¹/₂-inch-thick rounds**	Preheat the oven to 375° F.
2 **(4-ounce) packages goat cheese, cut into ¹/₄-inch slices**	Place the bread rounds on an ungreased 15x10x1-inch baking sheet. Bake for 15 minutes or until lightly browned. Top with goat cheese. Bake an additional 10 minutes or until cheese is soft.

Vanilla Ice Cream with Plum Compote

¹/₂ **cup sugar**

¹/₂ **cup water**

6 **ripe black or red plums, pitted and cut into ¹/₄-inch slices**

1¹/₂ **pints vanilla ice cream**

Bring sugar and water to a boil in a medium saucepan. Add the plums; return to a boil. Cook for 2 minutes. Reduce heat to low; cover and cook for 5 to 10 minutes or until plums are softened. Transfer the plums to a bowl with a slotted spoon; discard any loose peels. Cook the plum juices over high heat for 15 minutes or until thickened. Pour the syrup over plums; cool slightly.

Divide the ice cream among 6 dessert dishes; top with plum compote.

Makes 6 servings

TIP

Compote can be made up to 3 days ahead and stored, covered, in the refrigerator. Reheat in a saucepan before serving.

Traditional Tuna Salad

This is perfect comfort food for any time of year—
tuna salad and tomato soup.

2 (6-ounce) cans solid white tuna in water, drained

½ cup minced celery

6 to 7 tablespoons mayonnaise, to taste

1 teaspoon dried dill

¼ teaspoon salt

1 hard-cooked egg, peeled and chopped

Lettuce leaves

1 tomato, sliced

Combine the tuna, celery, mayonnaise, dill, salt, and egg in a large bowl; stir well. Refrigerate, covered, for at least 1 hour before serving. Arrange the lettuce leaves on 4 dinner plates; top with the tuna salad. Arrange the tomato slices on the side of the plate.

Makes 4 servings

TIP

Here are a few things to know when selecting canned tuna: Solid white tuna—usually Albacore, Yellow fin or Tongol tuna—is milder in flavor, has whiter meat and is packed in water. Light meat tuna—usually Skip Jacket or Bonito tuna—is stronger in flavor and darker in color. It is packed in oil or water. White tuna is usually more expensive and higher in calories, but many people prefer it.

Tomato Bisque

- 1 (14.5-ounce) can chicken broth
- 1 (14.5-ounce) can Italian stewed tomatoes
- 1 (8-ounce) can tomato sauce
- 1 (6-ounce) can tomato paste
- 1/4 cup chopped onion
- 1 tablespoon sugar
- 1 teaspoon Italian seasoning
- 1/2 teaspoon celery seed
- 1/4 teaspoon garlic powder
- 1/8 teaspoon ground white pepper
- 1 1/4 cups half-and-half

In a large saucepan, combine all the ingredients except the half-and-half; bring to a boil. Reduce heat and simmer, uncovered, for 15 minutes. Carefully pour the soup into the bowl of a food processor; pulse for 1 minute or until smooth. Return the soup to the saucepan. Stir in the half-and-half. Cook over low heat until soup is heated through.

Makes 4 servings

Dill Muffins

- 2 cups flour
- 1 tablespoon sugar
- 2 teaspoons baking powder
- 1/2 teaspoon salt
- 3 teaspoons dried dill
- 1/4 teaspoon freshly ground pepper
- 1 cup milk
- 1 cup small-curd cottage cheese
- 4 tablespoons melted butter
- 1 egg, lightly beaten
- 1 tablespoon minced onion

Preheat the oven to 400°F. Spray muffin cups with cooking spray.

Sift the flour, sugar, baking powder, and salt in a large bowl. Add the dill and pepper; stir to combine. Set aside.

Stir together the milk, cottage cheese, butter, egg, and onion in a bowl. Add the egg mixture to the flour mixture; stir with a wooden spoon until combined. Spoon the batter into the prepared muffin cups. Bake for 15 minutes or until a wooden pick inserted into the center comes out clean. Cool in the pan on a wire rack for 5 minutes. Remove the muffins from the pan. Cool completely.

Makes 12 muffins

Tuna and Grape Salad

Sautéed tuna steaks joined by potatoes, grapes, and a mustard vinaigrette dressing make a scrumptious meal.

Menu — Tuna and Grape Salad • Whole Wheat Muffins (See recipe on page 81) • Potent Strawberries

5 small red potatoes, cut into ¹/₂-inch cubes

3 tuna steaks (6 ounces each)

¹/₄ teaspoon salt

¹/₄ teaspoon pepper

1 tablespoon olive oil

¹/₄ cup minced fresh parsley

3 tablespoons white vinegar

3 tablespoons water

3 teaspoons Dijon mustard

3 tablespoons extra-virgin olive oil

¹/₂ teaspoon salt

¹/₄ teaspoon pepper

2 cups seedless red grapes, cut into halves

Romaine lettuce leaves

Place the potatoes in a medium-sized saucepan and cover with water by 1 inch. Bring to a boil over medium heat and cook for 12 to 15 minutes or until tender; drain. Set aside to cool.

Sprinkle the tuna with ¹/₄ teaspoon salt and ¹/₄ teaspoon pepper. Sear both sides of the tuna in 1 tablespoon olive oil in a large skillet over medium-high heat. Cover and cook, turning once, for 5 to 8 minutes, until tuna is light pink in the center or reaches desired degree of doneness (medium-rare is very pink in the center; medium is light pink in the center; well-done is evenly colored throughout). Set the tuna aside to cool; break into chunks.

Whisk together the parsley, vinegar, water, mustard, 3 table-spoons extra-virgin olive oil, ¹/₂ teaspoon salt, and ¹/₄ teaspoon pepper in a large bowl. Add the potatoes, tuna, and grapes; toss gently to coat. Arrange the lettuce leaves on 4 dinner plates; top with the salad. Serve at room temperature. Refrigerate leftovers.

Makes 4 servings

Potent Strawberries

1 pint vanilla ice cream

1 ¹/₂ cups sliced fresh strawberries

4 tablespoons Scotch whisky or orange-flavored liqueur (Grand Marnier)

Spoon ice cream into 4 dessert dishes; top with sliced strawberries. Drizzle with Scotch or liqueur.

Makes 4 servings

Meatless

Artichoke and Bean Pasta Salad

A fresh dill and basil vinaigrette complements fresh green beans, tomatoes, mozzarella cheese, kidney beans, and artichoke hearts in this yummy pasta salad.

3 cups green beans, trimmed and cut into 2-inch pieces

4 cups cooked rotini pasta

2 cups cherry tomato halves

2 cups cubed mozzarella cheese

1 (15-ounce) can kidney beans, rinsed and drained

1 (14-ounce) can quartered artichoke hearts, drained

1/3 cup extra-virgin olive oil

1/4 cup chopped fresh dill

1/4 cup chopped fresh basil

2 tablespoons red wine vinegar

1 teaspoon salt

1/2 teaspoon pepper

Place the green beans in the steamer basket of a medium saucepan over 1 inch of water; bring to a boil. Cover and steam for 5 minutes or until crisp-tender; drain and rinse with cold water.

Combine the green beans, pasta, tomatoes, cheese, kidney beans, and artichoke hearts in a large bowl. Whisk together the oil, dill, basil, vinegar, salt, and pepper in a small bowl. Pour the dressing over the pasta mixture; toss to coat. Refrigerate for at least 2 hours before serving.

Makes 6 servings

TIP

Dried herbs should not be substituted for fresh in the vinaigrette for this recipe.

Pear Squares

1 ½ **cups flour**

1 **cup old-fashioned oats**

1 **cup packed light brown sugar**

1 **teaspoon baking powder**

½ **teaspoon salt**

½ **teaspoon cinnamon**

¼ **teaspoon ground nutmeg**

¼ **cup milk**

3 **tablespoons vegetable oil**

3 **Bartlett pears, peeled, cored, and diced**

½ **cup walnuts, chopped**

Preheat the oven to 350°F. Spray a 9x9x2-inch baking pan with cooking spray.

Combine the flour, oats, brown sugar, baking powder, salt, cinnamon, and nutmeg in a large bowl. Add the milk and oil; stir with a fork until coarse crumbs form. Firmly press 2 cups of the oat mixture onto the bottom of the prepared pan. Top with the pears. Stir the walnuts into the remaining oat mixture; sprinkle evenly over the pears.

Bake for 30 minutes or until lightly browned. Cool completely in the pan on a wire rack. Cut into 16 squares.

Makes 16 squares

Asian Noodle Salad

Fresh vegetables and Chinese egg noodles are tossed
with a sesame dressing for this delightful meatless salad.

12 large dried shiitake mushrooms

1 (16-ounce) package fresh Chinese egg noodles

1 head napa cabbage, thinly sliced

2 tablespoons peanut oil, divided

1 yellow squash, thinly sliced

1/2 pound fresh snow peas, tips pinched off

1 teaspoon minced garlic

3 tablespoons sesame oil

1 tablespoon soy sauce

1 tablespoon rice vinegar

1 tablespoon minced fresh ginger root

1 teaspoon sugar

3 hard-cooked eggs, peeled and chopped

5 green onions, sliced

2 tablespoons chopped fresh cilantro

1/2 teaspoon salt

1/4 teaspoon pepper

Place the mushrooms in a medium bowl; add enough boiling water to cover. Let stand for 45 minutes or until the mushrooms are softened; drain. Cut off stems and discard; thinly slice caps.

Cook the noodles according to package directions; drain. Place the noodles in a large bowl.

Sauté the cabbage in 1 tablespoon peanut oil over medium-high heat for 3 to 4 minutes or until cabbage is wilted; set aside. In the same skillet, sauté mushrooms, squash, snow peas, and garlic in remaining peanut oil over medium-high heat for 2 minutes or until vegetables are crisp-tender. Add the vegetables to the noodles.

Whisk together the sesame oil, soy sauce, vinegar, ginger, and sugar in a small bowl. Pour the dressing over the noodles and vegetables; toss to coat. Sprinkle with the eggs, onions, cilantro, salt, and pepper; mix well. Serve at room temperature. *(Can be made 1 day ahead. Cover and refrigerate. Toss before serving.)*

Makes 4 servings

TIPS

Shiitake mushrooms and fresh Chinese egg noodles can be found in the produce section of your local supermarket.

Baby portobello mushrooms can be substituted for the shiitake mushrooms. There is no need to soak them in boiling water. Simply slice and sauté them with the squash and snow peas.

Asian Noodle Salad

Cheddar Cheese Biscuits

Caramelized Pineapple Parfaits (See recipe on page 47)

Cheddar Cheese Biscuits

- 2 **cups sifted flour**
- 2 **teaspoons baking powder**
- 1 **teaspoon sugar**
- ³/4 **teaspoon salt**
- ¹/2 **teaspoon baking soda**
- 6 **tablespoons butter, cold and cut into small pieces**
- 1 **cup heavy cream**
- 1 **cup shredded Cheddar cheese**

Preheat the oven to 450°F. Spray a 15x10x1-inch baking sheet with cooking spray.

Combine the flour, baking powder, sugar, salt, and baking soda in a large bowl. Cut in the butter with a pastry blender or 2 knives until the mixture resembles coarse crumbs. Add the cream and cheese, stirring with a fork. The dough will be very dry and crumbly. Finish incorporating the cream and cheese into the dry ingredients by kneading lightly with your hands. Work quickly and don't overmix.

Turn the dough out onto a lightly floured surface. Gently pat the dough to a 1-inch thickness. Cut out biscuits with a 2-inch round biscuit cutter, gathering and reshaping the scraps to make a total of 12 biscuits. Place the biscuits 1 inch apart on the prepared baking sheet. Bake for 10 to 15 minutes or until a wooden pick inserted into the center comes out clean. Cool on a wire rack. Serve warm.

Makes 12 biscuits

TIPS

For flaky biscuits, combine ingredients quickly and don't overmix.

Baked biscuits can be frozen for up to a month.

Egg Salad with Vegetables

Traditional egg salad becomes a delightful meal when stuffed inside a ripe, red tomato and accompanied by vegetables and delectable scones.

3/4 **pound green beans, trimmed**

3 **large carrots,**
   cut into 2x1/4-inch strips

8 **hard-cooked eggs,**
   peeled and chopped

1/2 **cup minced celery**

6 **tablespoons mayonnaise**

2 **teaspoons chopped fresh dill**

1/8 **teaspoon salt**

   Dash pepper

4 **medium ripe tomatoes**
   Lettuce leaves

Place the green beans and carrots in the steamer basket of a large saucepan over 1 inch of water; bring to a boil. Cover and steam for 6 to 8 minutes or until crisp-tender; drain and rinse with cold water. Set aside.

Combine the eggs, celery, mayonnaise, dill, salt, and pepper in a medium bowl. Refrigerate until ready to serve.

Remove the cores from the tomatoes. Slice the tomatoes into quarters, without cutting all the way through, and gently separate the quarters to make a tomato "flower." Line 4 plates with the lettuce leaves and top each one with a tomato. Fill the tomatoes with the egg salad. Arrange the green beans and carrots on the plates around the tomatoes.

Makes 4 servings

TIP

For perfect hard-cooked eggs, cover the eggs with cold water by about 1 inch in a large saucepan. Heat the water, uncovered, watching for the first large bubbles to rise to the surface. Reduce heat to keep the water just below the boiling point. Cook for 10 minutes. At 10 minutes, remove one egg and quickly shell it under cold running water. Slice the egg into halves; check the yolk. If the yolk is cooked through, remove the remaining eggs from the pan. If not, cook the eggs a minute or two longer. Carefully drain the hot water and place the pan in the sink under cold running water. When the eggs are cool enough to handle, peel the eggs and refrigerate until cooled.

Currant Scones

2 **cups flour**

¹/₄ **cup sugar**

1 ¹/₂ **teaspoons baking powder**

¹/₂ **teaspoon baking soda**

¹/₄ **teaspoon salt**

5 **tablespoons butter, cold and cut into small pieces**

¹/₂ **cup dried currants**

1 **egg, lightly beaten**

1 **cup buttermilk**

1 **egg white, lightly beaten**

¹/₂ **teaspoon sugar**

Preheat the oven to 425°F. Spray a 15x10x1-inch baking sheet with cooking spray.

Combine the flour, ¹/₄ cup sugar, baking powder, baking soda, and salt in a large bowl. Cut in the butter with a pastry blender or 2 knives until the mixture resembles coarse crumbs. Mix in the currants. Combine the egg and buttermilk in a small bowl. Add the egg mixture to the flour mixture, stirring with a fork until a soft dough forms. Knead the dough in the bowl with your hands until the flour is incorporated. Turn the dough out onto a lightly floured surface. Gently pat the dough to a 7-inch circle; cut into 8 wedges.

Place the scones 1 inch apart on the prepared baking sheet. Brush with the egg white; sprinkle with ¹/₂ teaspoon sugar. Bake for 15 minutes or until a wooden pick inserted into the center comes out clean. Cool on a wire rack. Serve warm.

Makes 8 scones

Eggplant Salad with Creamy Parmesan Dressing

Crispy fried eggplant and caramelized onions make a tantalizing salad.

1 large eggplant,
  cut into ¼-inch slices

1 tablespoon salt

½ cup heavy cream

¼ cup grated Parmesan cheese

½ teaspoon garlic salt

¼ teaspoon celery salt

1 large onion, sliced

2 tablespoons olive oil

1 yellow pepper, sliced

2 eggs, lightly beaten

1 cup seasoned bread crumbs

3 to 4 tablespoons olive oil

8 cups mixed greens

Place two wire racks on baking sheets lined with paper towels. Sprinkle both sides of the eggplant slices with salt; place on wire racks. Let sit for 30 minutes; rinse and pat dry.

Meanwhile, combine cream, cheese, garlic salt, and celery salt in a small bowl; let sit at room temperature for 20 minutes. Refrigerate until ready to serve.

Cook the onion in 2 tablespoons oil in a large saucepan over medium heat for 5 to 6 minutes or until softened. Add the pepper and cook for 5 to 6 minutes or until the pepper is softened and the onion is lightly browned; keep warm.

Place the eggs and bread crumbs in separate shallow bowls. Dip the eggplant slices in the eggs and then dredge with the bread crumbs. Cook the eggplant in about 3 tablespoons oil either on a griddle or in batches in a skillet for 2 to 3 minutes a side or until browned. Add additional oil as needed.

Divide the greens among 4 dinner plates; top with the onion, pepper, and eggplant. Drizzle the dressing over the salads.

Makes 4 servings

TIPS

Salting eggplant extracts any bitterness and prevents it from absorbing excessive amounts of oil during frying.

American eggplant has an elongated pear-shaped appearance. It is almost black in color, with a green stem cap which encircles the top of the eggplant like the cap of an elf. Some smaller varieties are called Italian eggplant. Japanese or Asian eggplant is smaller, thinner, and has a purple skin with a leaf cap that may be purple instead of green. Chinese white eggplant is similar in size to the Japanese eggplant.

Baked Apples

¹/₂ **cup (1 stick) butter, melted**

¹/₄ **cup dark rum**

¹/₂ **cup apple juice**

¹/₂ **cup packed brown sugar**

¹/₄ **cup (¹/₂ stick) butter, melted**

1 **teaspoon cinnamon**

¹/₂ **cup pecans, finely chopped**

¹/₂ **cup raisins**

4 **large Golden Delicious or Granny Smith apples**

   Whipped cream, as a garnish

Preheat the oven to 350°F. Combine ¹/₂ cup melted butter, rum, and apple juice in an 8x8x2-inch baking dish; set aside.

Combine the brown sugar, ¹/₄ cup melted butter, and cinnamon in a small bowl. Stir in the pecans and raisins; set aside.

Peel the skin off the top half of each apple. Scoop out the stems and cores with a melon baller, being careful not to cut through the bottoms. Cut a thin slice from the bottom of each apple to create a stable base. Place the apples upright in the prepared baking dish. Pack the cavities to the top with the pecan mixture. Spoon some of the liquid in the pan over the apples and filling.

Bake for about 45 minutes or until the apples are tender, basting often with the juices. Cover loosely with foil during baking if the filling browns too quickly. Serve warm garnished with whipped cream.

Makes 4 servings

TIP

Assemble this recipe before you start preparing the salad. Then put it in the oven just before you are ready to serve the salad.

Feel free to vary the ingredients in the filling to suit your taste.

Greek Salad

Paired with spinach and cheese triangles, this classic salad of crisp lettuce, tomatoes, olives, feta cheese, and lemon-mint vinaigrette makes a satisfying meal.

1/2 cup fresh lemon juice

2/3 cup extra-virgin olive oil

1 teaspoon dried oregano

1/4 cup minced fresh mint

1 garlic clove, minced

1/4 teaspoon salt

1 head iceberg lettuce, torn into bite-size pieces

1 cucumber, cut into 1/4-inch-thick slices; slices cut into halves

3 ripe tomatoes, cut into wedges

1/4 cup thinly sliced red onion

12 ounces feta cheese, cut into 1/4-inch cubes

1 (7-ounce) package Kalamata olives, drained

Whisk together the lemon juice, oil, oregano, mint, garlic, and salt in a small bowl. Refrigerate for at least 1/2 hour before serving.

Combine the lettuce, cucumber, tomatoes, onion, cheese, and olives in a large bowl. Pour the dressing over the salad; toss to coat.

Makes 6 servings

TIPS

Starting with cold ingredients makes this salad especially tasty.

NOTES

Feta cheese is believed to be one of the first cheeses ever produced. Although it was originally made with goat's or sheep's milk, it is now made with cow's milk. Feta has a firm, crumbly texture and can be salty, since it is preserved in brine. It is sold in solid blocks or already crumbled. This recipe calls for a solid block of feta cheese.

Farmer cheese, used in the spinach triangles, is merely a form of cottage cheese from which most of the liquid has been pressed. Very dry farmer cheese is available in solid loaves. It is easily sliced or crumbled, depending upon its age.

Spinach and Cheese Triangles (Spanakopita)

4 ounces cream cheese, softened

2 eggs

1 (10-ounce) package frozen chopped spinach, thawed and squeezed dry

½ cup crumbled feta cheese

½ cup crumbled farmer cheese

½ cup chopped fresh parsley

½ cup chopped fresh dill

¼ cup chopped green onions

2 tablespoons grated Parmesan cheese

8 ounces phyllo dough, thawed

1 cup butter, melted

Preheat the oven to 375°F. Spray three 15x10x1-inch baking pans with cooking spray.

Beat the cream cheese and eggs in a large bowl with an electric mixer at high speed until well blended. Add the spinach, feta cheese, farmer cheese, parsley, dill, onions, and Parmesan cheese; stir to combine.

Remove the phyllo dough from the wrapper; unfold and cover with a damp dish towel. Work with one sheet of dough at a time and keep remaining sheets covered with the damp towel. Carefully place 1 sheet of dough on a piece of waxed paper. Brush the sheet with melted butter; fold the sheet in half lengthwise. Arrange the dough vertically in front of you. Center a heaping teaspoonful of the cheese mixture about ½ inch from the bottom edge of the dough. Leading with a bottom corner, fold the dough up and over the filling, creating a triangle. Continue folding the dough over and over, making triangular folds. Cut off any excess dough at the end in order to keep the seam side on the bottom. Continue to make triangles with the remaining sheets of dough. Place the triangles on the prepared baking pans; brush the tops with melted butter. Bake for 18 to 20 minutes or until golden brown. Serve warm.

Makes 20 to 26 pieces

TIPS

The triangles can be prepared in advance, stored in the refrigerator or freezer, and then baked. Leftovers can be stored in the refrigerator and reheated in the oven. This recipe is based on 9x14-inch sheets of phyllo dough.

Grilled Vegetable Salad

Vegetables brushed with an herb-infused olive oil and grilled make a refreshing summertime meal.

1 cup extra-virgin olive oil

1 tablespoon minced fresh rosemary

1 tablespoon minced fresh oregano

1 tablespoon minced fresh thyme

2 garlic cloves, peeled

1 eggplant, cut into ¹/₂-inch slices

1 tablespoon salt

2 heads Belgian endive, cut in half lengthwise

2 large portobello mushroom caps

1 zucchini, cut lengthwise into ¹/₄-inch slices

1 yellow squash, cut lengthwise into ¹/₄-inch slices

1 onion, cut into ¹/₄-inch slices

Salt and pepper, to taste

¹/₄ cup extra-virgin olive oil

5 teaspoons balsamic vinegar

Pinch salt

8 cups mixed greens

Combine 1 cup oil, rosemary, oregano, thyme, and garlic in a small bowl; let the marinade sit at room temperature for at least 3 hours before using.

Place two wire racks on baking sheets lined with paper towels. Sprinkle both sides of the eggplant slices with 1 tablespoon salt; place on wire racks. Let sit for 30 minutes; rinse and pat dry.

Prepare a medium-hot fire in a charcoal or gas grill; oil the grill grate with cooking spray.

Using a pastry brush, baste all of the prepared vegetables with the marinade; season with salt and pepper. Grill the vegetables for 3 to 5 minutes a side or until browned.

Whisk together ¹/₄ cup oil, vinegar, and pinch of salt in a small bowl.

Divide the greens among 4 dinner plates; top with the grilled vegetables. Drizzle the dressing over the salads.

Makes 4 servings

TIPS

Leave the root end on the Belgian endive to keep the leaves together, but remember to wash it carefully. Swirl the endive in a large bowl with cold running water and gently pull the leaves slightly apart. Let the endive soak for a few minutes. The dirt should sink to the bottom of the bowl. Dry the endive thoroughly.

Trim the ends off of the eggplant, zucchini, and squash before slicing.

Thread the onion slices onto skewers to keep them from falling apart on the grill.

Grilled Vegetable Salad

Grilled French Bread

Rice Pudding

Grilled French Bread

1 mini-loaf French bread (about 12 inches long)

3 tablespoons butter, softened

Cut the bread in half horizontally. Spread the butter on the cut sides of the bread. Place the bread on a hot grill grate, buttered side down, and grill for 1 to 2 minutes or until golden brown. Cut into halves.

Makes 4 pieces

Rice Pudding

4 1/2 cups milk

2/3 cup long-grain white rice

1/3 cup sugar

1/8 teaspoon salt

1/3 cup dried cherries

1 1/2 teaspoons vanilla extract

Combine the milk, rice, sugar, and salt in a medium heavy saucepan. Bring to a simmer over medium heat, stirring occasionally. Reduce heat to medium-low. Simmer, uncovered, for 40 minutes or until rice is tender and creamy, adding the cherries during the last 15 minutes. Remove from heat; stir in the vanilla. Cover and refrigerate for at least 4 hours before serving.

Makes 6 servings

Italian Chopped Salad

Creamy buttermilk-basil dressing livens up crisp lettuce, vegetables, and beans in this easy-to-assemble salad.

1 small garlic clove, mashed

¹/₄ teaspoon salt

1¹/₃ cups buttermilk

²/₃ cup mayonnaise

¹/₄ cup minced fresh basil

1 large head iceberg lettuce, chopped

4 hard-cooked eggs, peeled and diced

2 ripe tomatoes, chopped

1 fennel bulb, chopped

1 (15-ounce) can cannellini beans, rinsed and drained

1 cup sliced fresh mushrooms

1 (7-ounce) jar roasted red peppers, drained and sliced

1 cup cubed Muenster cheese

1 (2.25-ounce) can sliced ripe olives, drained

Mash the garlic and salt to make a paste. Whisk together the garlic paste, buttermilk, mayonnaise, and basil in a medium bowl. Cover and refrigerate for 1 hour before serving.

Divide the lettuce among 4 dinner plates. Arrange the eggs, tomatoes, fennel, beans, mushrooms, peppers, cheese, and olives on top of the lettuce. *(For a nice presentation, arrange the ingredients in rows in the order listed.)* Drizzle the dressing over the salads.

Makes 4 servings

TIP

For perfect hard-cooked eggs, cover the eggs with cold water by about 1 inch in a large saucepan. Heat the water, uncovered, watching for the first large bubbles to rise to the surface. Reduce heat to keep the water just below the boiling point. Cook for 10 minutes. At 10 minutes, remove one egg and quickly shell it under cold running water. Slice the egg into halves; check the yolk. If the yolk is cooked through, remove the remaining eggs from the pan. If not, cook the eggs a minute or two longer. Carefully drain the hot water and place the pan in the sink under cold running water. When the eggs are cool enough to handle, peel the eggs and refrigerate until cooled.

Lemon Parfaits

1 (3-ounce) package cream cheese, softened

1 (11.25-ounce) jar lemon curd

1 cup whipped cream

3/4 cup coarsely crushed short-bread or vanilla wafer cookies

2 cups fresh berries (fresh raspberries, blueberries, or sliced strawberries)

1/4 cup chopped pistachio nuts

Beat the cream cheese in a medium bowl with an electric mixer at high speed until smooth. Add the lemon curd; beat at high speed until smooth. Fold in the whipped cream with a spatula just until combined. Cover and refrigerate until ready to serve. *(Can be made up to 1 day ahead.)*

To assemble, spoon 1 tablespoon cookie crumbs into each of 4 parfait glasses. Top with 1/4 cup lemon cream and 1/4 cup berries. Repeat layers. Sprinkle the tops of the parfaits with the nuts. *(Can be assembled up to 4 hours ahead. Cover and refrigerate until ready to serve.)*

Makes 4 servings

TIP

You can substitute almost any type of cookies and nuts that you have on hand.

Lentils with Vegetables

Lentils and vegetables team up with a spinach and goat cheese tart to make a scrumptious meal.

2 cups vegetable broth

1 cup dried lentils, rinsed and drained

¹/₂ cup diced carrot

¹/₂ cup diced onion

2 cups cauliflower florets

2 cups broccoli florets

1 zucchini, diced

1 red pepper, diced

1 teaspoon salt

¹/₂ teaspoon black pepper

¹/₄ cup fresh lemon juice

2 tablespoons olive oil

2 teaspoons sugar

¹/₂ teaspoon curry powder

2 tablespoons chopped fresh parsley

2 small heads Boston lettuce

Bring the broth, lentils, carrot, and onion to a boil in a medium saucepan. Reduce heat to medium-low; cover and simmer for 25 minutes or until lentils are tender. Drain and cool.

Meanwhile, place the cauliflower and broccoli in the steamer basket of a medium saucepan over 1 inch of water; bring to a boil. Cover and steam for 5 to 8 minutes or until crisp-tender; drain and rinse with cold water.

Combine the lentil mixture, cauliflower, broccoli, zucchini, red pepper, salt, and black pepper in a large bowl. Whisk together the lemon juice, oil, sugar, curry powder, and parsley in a small bowl. Pour the dressing over the vegetable mixture; toss to coat. Divide the lettuce among 4 dinner plates; top with the salad.

Makes 4 servings

TIP

There are several varieties of lentils—green, brown, red, yellow, and *verte du puy*. They are hard even when fresh so they are always sold dried. Lentils do not require presoaking like dried beans and take between 20 and 40 minutes of cooking to soften.

Delicious Salad Meals

Spinach and Goat Cheese Tart

Dough

- 3/4 **cup all-purpose flour**
- 1/2 **cup whole wheat flour**
- 1/2 **teaspoon salt**
- 6 **tablespoons butter, cold and cut into small pieces**
- 1 **(3-ounce) package cream cheese, softened**
- 1 **egg**

Topping

- 1 **medium onion, sliced**
- 2 **tablespoons olive oil, divided**
- 1 **(7-ounce) package spinach**
- 1 **(14-ounce) package crumbled goat cheese**
- 3 **tablespoons heavy cream**
- 1/8 **teaspoon ground nutmeg**
- 2 **tablespoons golden raisins**
- 1 **tablespoon pine nuts**
- 1 **egg white, beaten**

To make the crust: Process the flours and salt in a food processor until blended. Add the butter; pulse until the mixture resembles coarse crumbs. Add the cream cheese and egg; pulse just until moist clumps form. Do not overprocess. Gather the dough into a ball; flatten into a disk. Wrap the dough in plastic wrap; refrigerate for at least 1 hour.

Preheat the oven to 400°F.

To make the topping: Sauté the onion in 1 tablespoon oil in a large skillet for 15 minutes or until lightly browned; remove from skillet. In the same skillet, sauté spinach in remaining oil for 1 to 2 minutes or until wilted. Combine the goat cheese, cream, and nutmeg in a small bowl, mashing with a fork until smooth.

To assemble the tart: Roll out the dough to an 11-inch circle between 2 sheets of parchment paper. Remove the top sheet of parchment paper; slide the dough onto a baking sheet, keeping the bottom parchment in place. Arrange the onion over the dough, spreading to within 2 inches of the edge. Drop the goat cheese mixture by tablespoonfuls over the onion; sprinkle with the raisins. Top with the spinach; sprinkle with the pine nuts.

Fold the outer edge of the dough over the filling, using the parchment paper as an aid. Overlap the dough slightly while folding and press gently to seal. (The dough will only partially cover the filling.) Brush the dough with the egg white. Bake for 30 minutes or until the pastry is golden brown. Cool on a wire rack for 10 minutes. Serve warm or at room temperature. Cut into 8 wedges.

Makes 8 pieces

Mexican Salad

You won't even miss the meat or chicken in this salad, because there are plenty of vegetables and beans filling the layers.

½ **cup refried beans**

½ **cup sour cream**

1 **tablespoon taco seasoning mix**

4 **tostada shells**

8 **cups chopped iceberg lettuce**

1 **(15-ounce) can black beans, rinsed and drained**

2 **large ripe tomatoes, chopped**

2 **cups whole corn kernels, fresh; canned and drained; or frozen and thawed**

4 **tablespoons chopped ripe olives**

1 **cup shredded Mexican cheese**

1 **avocado, peeled and diced**

1 **(8-ounce) jar taco sauce**

Mix the refried beans, sour cream, and taco seasoning mix in a small bowl until combined. Heat the tostada shells according to the package directions. Place each of the warmed shells on a dinner plate. Spoon ¼ cup of the refried bean mixture into each shell. Divide the lettuce among the 4 shells; top with the black beans, tomatoes, corn, and olives. Sprinkle with the cheese and the avocado. Serve the salads with the taco sauce as a dressing.

Makes 4 servings

TIPS

Serve tortilla chips on the side to scoop up the salad. Make more of the refried bean mixture and serve separately as a dip.

You also can serve this salad in tortilla shells which have been formed into a bowl.

Select avocados that yield to gentle pressure and store them in the refrigerator. If an avocado is firm, ripen at room temperature for several days or, more quickly, in a closed paper bag.

To pit an avocado, do not remove the skin. Cut the avocado in half down to the pit. Twist the halves to separate. Holding the half with the pit in one hand, carefully strike the pit with the blade of a sturdy knife to wedge the blade firmly into the pit. Twist and lift the knife to remove the pit.

To scoop out and slice or dice an avocado, slide a large spoon between the avocado flesh and the skin. Scoop out the flesh in one piece. Place it, cut side down, on a work surface. Slice with a small knife. Cut across the slices to dice the avocado to the desired size.

Rustic Cherry Tart

1 1/3 **cups flour**

1/3 **cup cornmeal**

3 **tablespoons sugar**

1/4 **teaspoon salt**

1/2 **cup (1 stick) butter, cold and cut into small pieces**

4 **tablespoons ice water**

3 **(15-ounce) cans Bing cherries, drained**

1 **teaspoon almond extract**

2 **tablespoons sugar**

1 **egg, beaten**

1 **teaspoon sugar**

Vanilla ice cream (optional)

Combine the flour, cornmeal, 3 tablespoons sugar, and salt in a medium bowl. Cut in the butter with a pastry blender or 2 knives until the mixture resembles coarse crumbs. Sprinkle the water over the flour mixture; gently toss with a fork. Add a little more water, if necessary, until the flour is moistened. Knead the dough in the bowl 4 or 5 times, until all the flour is incorporated. Gather the dough into a ball; flatten into a disk. Wrap the dough in plastic wrap; refrigerate for 1 hour.

Preheat the oven to 425°F.

Combine the cherries and almond extract in a large bowl. Sprinkle with 2 tablespoons sugar and toss to coat; set aside.

Roll out the dough to a 13-inch round between 2 sheets of parchment paper. Remove and discard the top paper. Slide the dough onto a baking sheet, keeping the bottom paper in place. Using a slotted spoon, transfer the cherry mixture to the center of the dough, spreading to within 2 inches of the edge; reserve any juice. Fold the outer edge of the dough over the cherries using the parchment paper as an aid. Overlap the dough slightly while folding and press gently to seal. (The dough will only partially cover the cherries.) If the dough tears, press it back together. Whisk the egg in a small bowl. Brush the egg over the dough and sprinkle the dough and fruit with 1 teaspoon sugar. Pour the reserved juice over the cherries.

Bake for 35 to 45 minutes or until the pastry is browned and the cherries are bubbling. Cool for about 30 minutes on the baking sheet on a wire rack. Serve warm with vanilla ice cream, if desired.

Makes 8 servings

Middle Eastern Salad

A lemon vinaigrette deliciously accents nutty bulgur wheat, chickpeas, cucumber, tomatoes, feta cheese, and pine nuts in this delectable dish.

3 cups vegetable broth

1 1/2 cups uncooked bulgur wheat

1 (15-ounce) can chickpeas or garbanzo beans, rinsed and drained

1 cup peeled and chopped cucumber

1/2 cup chopped celery

6 green onions, sliced

2 cups halved cherry tomatoes

6 tablespoons extra-virgin olive oil

2 tablespoons fresh lemon juice

3 teaspoons chopped fresh dill or 1 teaspoon dried dill

1/2 teaspoon salt

1/2 teaspoon pepper

1 (4-ounce) package crumbled feta cheese

1/2 cup pine nuts, toasted

Bring the broth and bulgur to a boil in a large saucepan. Reduce heat; cover and simmer for 22 to 25 minutes or until liquid is absorbed and the bulgur is tender. Transfer the bulgur to a large non-reactive bowl; cool to room temperature. Add the chickpeas, cucumber, celery, onions, and tomatoes; mix to combine. Whisk together the oil, lemon juice, dill, salt, and pepper in a small bowl. Pour the dressing over the salad; toss to coat. Fold in the cheese and pine nuts. Refrigerate for at least 2 hours before serving.

Makes 6 servings

TIP

Bulgur wheat is made from cooked wheat berries which have the bran removed and are then dried and crushed. This light grain cooks quickly and has a nutty taste. It can be found in the natural food section of your local supermarket.

Cheese Triangles (Boereg)

1 (8-ounce) package cream cheese, softened

2 eggs

2 (8-ounce) packages Muenster cheese, coarsely grated

1/4 cup chopped fresh dill

8 ounces phyllo dough, thawed

1 cup butter, melted

Preheat the oven to 375°F. Spray three 15x10x1-inch baking pans with cooking spray.

Beat the cream cheese and eggs in a large bowl with an electric mixer at high speed until well blended. Stir in the cheese and dill by hand until combined.

Remove the phyllo dough from the wrapper; unfold and cover with a damp dish towel. Work with one sheet of dough at a time and keep remaining sheets covered with the damp towel. Carefully place 1 sheet of dough on a piece of waxed paper. Brush the sheet with melted butter; fold the sheet in half lengthwise. Arrange the dough vertically in front of you. Center a heaping teaspoonful of the cheese mixture about 1/2 inch from the bottom edge of the dough. Leading with a bottom corner, fold the dough up and over the filling, creating a triangle. Continue folding the dough over and over, making triangular folds. Cut off any excess dough at the end in order to keep the seam side on the bottom. Continue to make triangles with the remaining sheets of dough. Place the triangles on the prepared baking pans; brush the tops with melted butter. Bake for 18 to 20 minutes or until golden brown. Serve warm.

Makes 20 to 26 pieces

TIPS

The triangles can be prepared in advance, stored in the refrigerator or freezer, and then baked. Leftovers can be stored in the refrigerator and reheated in the oven.

This recipe is based on 9x14-inch sheets of phyllo dough.

Napa Cabbage Salad

*Buttery, crunchy noodles are tossed with napa cabbage
and other vegetables in this Asian-inspired salad.*

2 (3-ounce) packages Oriental-
  flavored ramen noodle soup

½ cup butter

½ cup slivered almonds

1 tablespoon sesame seeds

⅔ cup peanut or vegetable oil

3 tablespoons rice vinegar

2 teaspoons sugar

1 teaspoon soy sauce

1 large head napa cabbage, thinly
  sliced

2 cups shredded carrots

2 cups frozen peas, thawed

2 (8-ounce) cans whole baby
  sweet corn, drained

1 (8-ounce) can sliced water
  chestnuts, drained

¼ cup chopped green onions

Break the ramen noodles into small pieces, reserving the seasoning pack for another use. Melt the butter over medium
heat in a large skillet. Add the noodles, almonds, and sesame
seeds; cook for 5 to 7 minutes, stirring constantly, until the
noodles are lightly browned. Remove from heat and cool to
room temperature.

Whisk together the oil, vinegar, sugar, and soy sauce in a
small bowl; set aside.

Combine the cabbage, carrots, peas, baby corn, water chestnuts, and onions in a very large bowl; add the noodle mixture. Pour the dressing over the salad; toss well.

Makes 8 servings

TIPS

Napa cabbage, otherwise known as Chinese cabbage, has
white ribs and veiny green leaves. It's commonly used in
Asian cooking and can be found year-round in the produce
section of your local supermarket.

To save preparation time, purchase shredded carrots.

Mushroom Tart

Crust

1 ¹/₂ **cups flour**

1 **tablespoon chopped fresh thyme**

¹/₂ **teaspoon salt**

6 **tablespoons butter, cold and cut into small pieces**

3 **tablespoons shortening, cold**

4 **tablespoons ice water**

Filling

1 **(8-ounce) package sliced mushrooms**

1 **tablespoon olive oil**

3 **eggs**

¹/₂ **cup milk**

¹/₂ **cup heavy cream**

¹/₈ **teaspoon salt**

¹/₈ **teaspoon pepper**

To make the crust: Process the flour, thyme, and salt in a food processor until blended. Add the butter and shortening; pulse until the mixture resembles coarse crumbs. Add the water; pulse just until moist clumps form, adding a little more water, if necessary. Do not overprocess. Gather the dough into a ball; flatten into a disk. Wrap the dough in plastic wrap; refrigerate for 1 hour.

Spray a 9-inch tart pan with cooking spray. (If using a tart pan with a removable bottom, wrap the pan with foil before filling to prevent leaks.) Roll out the dough to a 12-inch circle on a lightly floured surface. Gently lift the dough just enough to move the prepared pan underneath it. Press the dough firmly onto the bottom and side of the pan. If there are places where the dough doesn't reach to the top of the pan, break off any excess dough and press it into place. Reinforce the seam where the bottom and side meet with excess dough. Pierce the bottom of the crust all over with a fork. Cover; freeze for 30 minutes. Preheat the oven to 400°F.

Place the crust on a baking sheet. Bake for 20 minutes or until lightly browned on the bottom. Cool for 5 minutes on a wire rack. *Reduce oven temperature to 375°F.*

To make the filling: Sauté the mushrooms in 1 tablespoon oil in a large skillet for 5 minutes or until lightly browned. Whisk together the eggs, milk, cream, salt, and pepper until combined; stir in the mushrooms. Pour the filling into the pre-baked crust. Bake for 25 minutes or until a wooden pick inserted into the center comes out clean. Cool on a wire rack. Serve warm or at room temperature. Refrigerate any leftovers.

Makes 6 servings

Roasted Vegetable Pasta Salad

The aroma of vegetables roasting in the oven will entice your family to the kitchen for this tasty salad.

1/2 cup olive oil

1 tablespoon minced fresh tarragon

1 small butternut squash, peeled and cut into 1-inch pieces

1 large zucchini, cut into 1-inch pieces

1 red pepper, cut into 1-inch pieces

1 medium onion, cut into 1-inch pieces

1 head cauliflower, cut into florets

3 carrots, sliced

3 cups cooked farfalle pasta

1/2 cup extra-virgin olive oil

2 tablespoons fresh lemon juice

2 tablespoons minced fresh parsley

2 tablespoons minced fresh basil

1 tablespoon minced fresh tarragon

1 teaspoon salt

1/2 teaspoon black pepper

1/2 cup shredded Parmesan cheese

Preheat the oven to 450°F. Spray a 15x10x1-inch baking sheet with cooking spray.

Whisk together 1/2 cup olive oil and 1 tablespoon tarragon in a small bowl; set aside. Arrange the squash, zucchini, red pepper, onion, cauliflower, and carrots on the prepared baking sheet. Drizzle the vegetables with the olive oil mixture. Bake for 30 minutes or until the vegetables are tender; cool to room temperature. Combine the pasta and vegetables in a large bowl.

Whisk together 1/2 cup extra-virgin olive oil, lemon juice, parsley, basil, 1 tablespoon tarragon, salt, and black pepper in a small bowl. Drizzle the dressing over the pasta and vegetables; toss to coat. Sprinkle the salad with the cheese; toss to coat. Serve at room temperature. Refrigerate any leftovers.

Makes 8 servings

TIPS

Add or substitute any of your favorite vegetables.

Tomatoes also can be added once the salad is assembled: 1 to 2 cups halved cherry tomatoes, or 1 cup chopped sun-dried tomatoes.

Bran Muffins

2 cups wheat bran
1 cup flour
1 teaspoon baking soda
1 teaspoon salt
1 1/4 cups milk
1/2 cup molasses
1 cup golden raisins

Preheat the oven to 350°F. Spray muffin cups with cooking spray.

Combine the wheat bran, flour, baking soda, and salt in a large bowl; set aside.

Stir together the milk and molasses in a small bowl. Add the milk mixture and raisins to the flour mixture; stir by hand until combined. Spoon the batter into the prepared muffin cups. Bake for 18 to 20 minutes or until a wooden pick inserted into the center comes out clean. Cool in the pan on a wire rack for 5 minutes. Remove the muffins from the pan. Serve warm.

Makes 12 muffins

TIP

You can find wheat bran in the health food section of your local supermarket.

Thai Noodle Salad

Serve yourself a treat from this large platter of lettuce, cabbage, Japanese noodles, crunchy vegetables, and spicy peanut dressing.

¹/₃ cup fresh lime juice

2 tablespoons minced fresh ginger root

3 tablespoons olive oil

3 tablespoons low-sodium soy sauce

¹/₄ cup creamy peanut butter

2 tablespoons honey

3 teaspoons Thai chili sauce

1 garlic clove, minced

1 (10-ounce) package Japanese udon noodles

6 cups sliced romaine lettuce

4 cups shredded green cabbage

2 cups coarsely shredded, peeled raw sweet potato

1 red pepper, thinly sliced

1 green pepper, thinly sliced

1 cup coarsely shredded, peeled daikon or red radishes

1 cup bean sprouts

¹/₄ cup chopped peanuts

Whisk together the lime juice, ginger, oil, soy sauce, peanut butter, honey, chili sauce, and garlic in a small bowl; set aside.

Cook the noodles according to package directions. Drain the noodles; rinse under cold water and drain again.

Combine the lettuce and cabbage in a large bowl; toss well. Spread the lettuce mixture over a large serving platter; top with the noodles in the center of the platter. Arrange individual mounds of the sweet potato, peppers, daikon, and bean sprouts around the noodles. Serve the dressing and the peanuts on the side.

Makes 6 servings

TIP

Udon noodles are Japanese wheat noodles. You can find them fresh in the produce section or dried in the ethnic section of your local supermarket.

Daikon are very long, white radishes that can weigh up to several pounds each. Americans are more familiar with the small, round, ruby-red variety of radish.

Buttermilk Biscuits

Purchase refrigerated biscuit dough and bake according to the package directions. Or, make the Buttermilk Biscuits on page 35.

Banana, Raspberry and Chocolate Cakes

6 ounces semisweet baking chocolate, chopped

2 tablespoons butter

1 (12-ounce) package frozen raspberries, thawed

1/2 cup (1 stick) butter, softened

3/4 cup sugar

2 eggs

1/4 cup milk

1 very ripe banana, mashed

1 teaspoon vanilla extract

1 cup flour

1/4 teaspoon salt

1 tablespoon sugar

Preheat the oven to 350°F. Grease 10 muffin cups.

Melt the chocolate and 2 tablespoons butter in a small heatproof bowl set over a saucepan of simmering water, stirring constantly until smooth. Remove the bowl from the pan; set aside to cool. Drain the raspberries, reserving the juice; set aside.

Beat 1/2 cup butter and 3/4 cup sugar in a large bowl with an electric mixer at high speed until well blended. Add the eggs, milk, banana, and vanilla; mix well. Stir in the flour and salt by hand. Gently fold in 3/4 cup of the drained raspberries. Spoon 1 heaping teaspoon of the batter into each muffin cup. Top with 1 teaspoon of the melted chocolate and another heaping teaspoon of the batter.

Bake for 20 minutes or until lightly browned around the edges. Cool in the muffin cups for 10 minutes. Run a small knife between the cakes and the sides of the cups. Remove from the cups to wire racks; cool slightly.

Process the remaining raspberries in a blender or food processor until puréed. Pour through a fine strainer set over a bowl to remove the seeds, pressing the purée through the strainer. Discard the seeds in the strainer. Add the reserved raspberry juice and 1 tablespoon sugar to the purée; stir to dissolve the sugar.

Place each warm cake on an individual plate. Pour the raspberry sauce around the cakes. Serve warm.

Makes 10 servings

Meatless

Vegetable and Rice Salad

Brown and wild rice join with crunchy vegetables, fruit, and nuts to make this tantalizing salad.

Menu   *Vegetable and Rice Salad* • *Bran Muffins* (See recipe on page 137)
Baked Apples (See recipe on page 121)

6 tablespoons extra-virgin olive oil

2 tablespoons balsamic vinegar

1 teaspoon salt

$^1/_2$ teaspoon Dijon mustard

$^1/_4$ teaspoon black pepper

3 cups cooked brown rice

1 $^1/_2$ cups cooked wild rice

2 cups seedless red grapes

1 cup frozen peas, thawed

1 red pepper, chopped

1 cup chopped pecans

2 stalks celery, sliced

1 Granny Smith apple, peeled, cored, and chopped

$^1/_4$ cup chopped red onion

Whisk together the oil, vinegar, salt, mustard, and black pepper in a small bowl. Combine the brown rice, wild rice, grapes, peas, red pepper, pecans, celery, apple, and onion in a large bowl. Pour the dressing over the salad; toss to coat. Cover and refrigerate for at least 4 hours before serving.

Makes 6 servings

TIP

Cooked wild rice can be found on the shelf with the rice at your local supermarket.

Salad Parties

Fall Football Party

Prepare all of these side-dish salads ahead of time
and enjoy watching the game!

Bratwurst and Italian Sausage

Grill your favorite brand of bratwurst and Italian sausage. Serve with all of the usual condiments, along with pickles, sauerkraut, and pepper rings. For faster grilling, precook the bratwurst and sausage in a large stockpot in beer and water for about 10 minutes.

Apple Cole Slaw

6 cups shredded green cabbage

1 1/2 cups shredded carrots

2 Granny Smith apples, peeled, cored, and chopped

4 green onions, sliced

2 tablespoons cider vinegar

1/2 cup sour cream

1/3 cup mayonnaise

2 tablespoons apple juice

1/2 teaspoon salt

1/8 teaspoon pepper

Combine the cabbage, carrots, apples, and onions in a large bowl. Add the vinegar; toss to coat. Whisk together the sour cream, mayonnaise, apple juice, salt, and pepper in a small bowl. Add the dressing to the cabbage mixture; toss to blend. Cover and refrigerate for at least 1 hour. Toss the salad to blend before serving.

Makes 10 servings

TIP

This salad can be made 1 day ahead.

 Party Tips

Serve potato chips with onion dip and tortilla chips
with guacamole, if you desire.

Be sure to break out the paper plates and plastic ware
to cut down on the cleanup.

Menu

Serves 10 to 12

Bratwurst and Italian Sausage
Apple Cole Slaw
Layered Lettuce Salad
German Potato Salad
Chocolate Sheet Cake

Layered Lettuce Salad

1 head iceberg lettuce, chopped

3 hard-cooked eggs, peeled and sliced

½ cup chopped onion

½ cup chopped green pepper

½ cup chopped celery

2 cups frozen green peas

1½ cups mayonnaise

1 cup grated Cheddar cheese

8 slices bacon, cooked crisp, drained, and crumbled

Place the lettuce in a 6-quart or large round, clear-glass bowl. Slide the egg slices between the lettuce and the inside of the bowl, placing them side by side around the circumference of the bowl. Layer the onion, pepper, celery, and peas on top of the lettuce. Spread the mayonnaise over the peas; sprinkle with the cheese and bacon. Do not stir. Cover and refrigerate overnight. Stir the salad immediately before serving.

Makes 10 servings

TIP

Plan to make this salad the day before. It needs to be refrigerated overnight.

Other chopped vegetables such as tomatoes and zucchini also can be added.

 Party Tip

Fire up the grill during the first half of the game so you can grill and serve the food just as the halftime show starts.

German Potato Salad

4 pounds Yukon gold potatoes, peeled and sliced ¼ inch thick

1 tablespoon salt

1 pound bacon, cut into ½-inch pieces

1 cup chopped onion

¼ cup flour

½ cup cider vinegar

1 (10.5-ounce) can beef broth

1 tablespoon sugar

½ teaspoon pepper

½ cup chopped fresh parsley

Place the potatoes in a large stockpot with enough water to cover by several inches. Bring to a boil over high heat; add 1 tablespoon salt. Reduce heat to medium to maintain a gentle boil. Cook for 8 minutes or until potatoes are tender when pierced with a knife; drain. Place the potatoes into a 13x9x2-inch baking dish; keep warm.

Meanwhile, cook the bacon in a large skillet until crispy; drain on paper towels. Discard all but 1 teaspoon of the drippings from the skillet. Add the onions; sauté for 5 minutes or until crisp-tender. Combine the bacon and onions with the potatoes.

Whisk together the flour and vinegar in a small bowl until smooth; set aside. Bring the broth, sugar, and pepper to a boil over medium heat in a small saucepan. Add the flour mixture; return to a boil and cook for 3 minutes or until thickened. Pour the hot dressing over the potatoes. Sprinkle with the parsley; toss to coat. Keep warm in a 200°F oven until ready to serve.

Makes 10 servings

TIP

Yellow-fleshed Yukon gold potatoes are richer and require less butter than their counterparts.

Party Tips

Offer several different types of beer—microbrews, dark beer, imports, as well as the usual brands—for everyone to choose from.

Chocolate Sheet Cake

Cake

- 2 cups flour
- 2 cups sugar
- 2 teaspoons cinnamon
- 1 teaspoon baking soda
- 1 cup (2 sticks) butter
- 1 cup water
- 2 tablespoons unsweetened cocoa
- 1/2 cup buttermilk
- 2 eggs
- 1 teaspoon vanilla extract

Frosting

- 1/2 cup (1 stick) butter, softened
- 6 tablespoons milk
- 4 tablespoons unsweetened cocoa
- 4 cups confectioners' sugar
- 1 cup chopped pecans
- 1 teaspoon vanilla extract

Preheat the oven to 350°F.

To make the cake: Sift together the flour, sugar, cinnamon, and baking soda in a large mixing bowl; set aside. Melt the butter in a medium saucepan over medium heat. Add the water and cocoa; bring to a boil. Remove from heat and pour into the flour mixture.

Beat with an electric mixer at medium speed until well blended. Add the buttermilk, eggs, and vanilla. Spread into a 15x10 1/2 x1-inch baking pan. Bake for 20 to 25 minutes or until a wooden pick inserted into the center comes out clean. Cool in the pan on a wire rack for 10 minutes.

To make the frosting: Heat the butter, milk, and cocoa in a medium saucepan over medium heat for 3 minutes or until the butter is melted. Add the confectioners' sugar, pecans, and vanilla. Cook and stir for 5 minutes or until the sugar is dissolved and the frosting is smooth; spread over the warm cake. Cool completely in the pan on a wire rack. Cut into squares.

Makes 24 pieces

Ladies' Luncheon

Cooked rotisserie chicken and vegetables drizzled with a creamy lemon dressing is just the beginning of this lovely, lemony luncheon for special friends.

Chicken Salad Platter

1 ⅓ cups sour cream

⅓ cup mayonnaise

1 tablespoon milk

Grated zest of 1 lemon

Juice of 1 lemon

1 garlic clove, crushed

⅛ teaspoon salt

⅛ teaspoon white pepper

1 pound fresh asparagus, trimmed

2 cooked rotisserie chickens

2 heads Boston lettuce, torn

4 hard-cooked eggs, peeled and sliced

2 mangoes, peeled, pitted, and sliced

Carrot Salad

Combine the sour cream, mayonnaise, milk, lemon zest, lemon juice, garlic, salt, and pepper in a small bowl. Cover and refrigerate until ready to serve. *(Can be made 1 day in advance.)*

Cook the asparagus in a large pot of boiling water for 2 to 3 minutes or until crisp-tender. Drain and rinse under cold water.

Remove the breast meat from the cooked chickens; cut into slices. Divide the lettuce among 6 dinner plates. Arrange the sliced chicken in the middle of the plate; drizzle with the lemon dressing. Arrange the asparagus, eggs, mangoes, and Carrot Salad *(recipe follows)* around the chicken.

Makes 6 servings

TIPS

You can purchase rotisserie chickens from your local supermarket, or grill 6 chicken breasts for this salad.

Instead of mangoes, you can use any fresh fruit—cantaloupe, seedless grapes, nectarines, or peaches—that you prefer.

Carrot Salad

¹/₂ **cup raisins**

2 **tablespoons minced fresh ginger root**

¹/₄ **cup white wine vinegar**

1 **tablespoon sugar**

1 **tablespoon fresh lemon juice**

³/₄ **cup sour cream**

3 **cups shredded carrots**

Combine the raisins, ginger, and vinegar; let sit for 20 minutes. Add the sugar and lemon juice; stir until sugar is dissolved. Add the sour cream; mix well. Combine the mixture with the carrots in a large bowl. Cover and refrigerate for at least 2 hours before serving.

Makes 6 servings

TIP

Purchasing shredded carrots in the produce section of your local supermarket makes this salad even easier to prepare.

 Party Tip

Serve champagne or sparkling grape juice in tall stemmed glasses garnished with fresh raspberries. Or, make white sangria. Add sliced oranges, lemons, limes, and kiwifruit to a pitcher of white wine. Let the sangria sit for an hour to blend the flavors. Add ice when you are ready to serve.

Cherry Lemon Muffins

2 cups flour

5 tablespoons sugar

2 teaspoons baking powder

1 teaspoon baking soda

1/2 teaspoon salt

1 cup buttermilk

5 tablespoons butter, melted

1 egg, lightly beaten

Grated zest of 1 lemon

Juice of 1 lemon

1 cup chopped dried cherries

Preheat the oven to 375°F. Spray muffin cups with cooking spray.

Combine the flour, sugar, baking powder, baking soda, and salt in a large bowl. Stir together the buttermilk, butter, egg, lemon zest and lemon juice in a small bowl. Add the milk mixture to the flour mixture; stir by hand until combined. Add the cherries; stir to combine. Spoon the batter into the prepared muffin cups. Bake for 18 to 20 minutes or until a wooden pick inserted into the center comes out clean. Cool in the pan on a wire rack for 5 minutes. Remove the muffins from the pan.

Makes 12 muffins

Lemon Cream Tart

Crust

1 1/2 cups flour

1/4 cup sugar

1/2 cup (1 stick) butter, cold and cut into small pieces

3 tablespoons milk

1 egg yolk

Lemon Cream

1 cup sugar

Grated zest of 3 lemons

4 eggs

3/4 cup fresh lemon juice

1 cup (2 sticks) butter, softened and cut into small pieces

Fresh strawberries, raspberries, or other fresh fruit, as a garnish

---

TIPS

The lemon cream can be made up to 4 days ahead and stored, covered, in the refrigerator.

The tart can be made up to 1 day ahead.

To make the crust: Process the flour and sugar in a food processor until blended. Add the butter. Pulse until the mixture resembles coarse crumbs. Whisk together the milk and egg yolk in a small bowl. With the processor on, slowly add the egg mixture, processing just until moist clumps form. Do not overprocess. Gather the dough into a ball; flatten into a disk. Wrap in plastic wrap; refrigerate for 1 hour. *(Pastry dough can be refrigerated for up to 3 days. Let the dough stand at room temperature to soften slightly before rolling.)*

Spray a 9-inch tart pan with a removable bottom with cooking spray. Roll out the dough to an 11-inch round between 2 sheets of parchment paper. Remove the top paper and invert the pastry into the tart pan. Remove the second paper. Press the dough firmly onto the bottom and side of the pan. If there are places where the dough doesn't reach to the top of the pan, break off any excess dough and press it into place. Reinforce the seam where the bottom and side meet with excess dough. Pierce the bottom of the crust all over with a fork. Cover; freeze for 30 minutes.

Preheat the oven to 350°F. Place the crust on a baking sheet. Bake for 20 minutes or until lightly browned. Cool completely on a wire rack. Gently loosen and remove the edge of the pan.

To make the lemon cream: Place the sugar and lemon zest in a heavy, medium saucepan; rub together with your fingers until the sugar is moist and very aromatic. Whisk in the eggs and lemon juice. Cook over medium-low heat, whisking constantly, for 15 minutes. Do not bring to a boil or the eggs will cook. (The mixture will begin to thicken after about 10 minutes, but continue cooking and whisking constantly for another 5 minutes.) Pour through a fine strainer set over a blender container. Add the butter. Blend until the butter is completely incorporated. Pour into the prepared crust. Cover and refrigerate for at least 4 hours. Serve garnished with fresh fruit.

Makes 8 servings

Mediterranean Barbecue

My husband's family introduced me to Armenian cooking and this is their traditional barbecue meal.

Lamb Shish Kebobs

4 **pounds boneless leg or shoulder of lamb, trimmed and cut into 1-inch cubes**

2 **onions, cut into quarters**

1 **green pepper, sliced**

1 **cup red wine**

¹/₂ **cup minced fresh parsley**

¹/₄ **cup olive oil**

2 **cups yogurt**

2 **garlic cloves, minced**

¹/₄ **teaspoon salt**

2 **onions, cut into quarters**

3 **green peppers, cut into large chunks**

Salt and black pepper, to taste

4 **(6- to 7-inch) pita bread rounds, cut into halves**

Place the lamb, 2 onions, and 1 green pepper in a large bowl. Combine the wine, parsley, and oil in another bowl. Pour the marinade over the meat mixture; toss to coat. Refrigerate overnight.

Combine the yogurt, garlic, and salt in a small bowl. Refrigerate at least 2 hours before serving. *(Can be made 1 day ahead.)*

Prepare a medium-hot fire in a charcoal or gas grill; oil the grill grate with cooking spray. Thread the remaining onions and green peppers onto skewers; grill for 5 to 10 minutes, turning to cook evenly and to prevent charring; keep warm.

Remove the meat from the bowl; discard the marinade. Season to taste with salt and black pepper.

Thread the lamb onto skewers; grill for 5 to 6 minutes a side over a medium-hot fire or until meat reaches desired doneness (medium-rare is very pink in the center; medium is light pink in the center; well-done is brown throughout). Serve the lamb in pita bread with the grilled onions and green peppers and the yogurt sauce.

Makes 8 servings

TIP

Substitute sirloin for the lamb, if you prefer.

Lamb Shish Kebobs
Tabbouleh
Rice Pilaf
Hummus (See recipe on page 63)
Boereg (See recipe on page 133)
Paklava

Tabbouleh

1 cup fine (No. 1) bulgur wheat

1 ¹/₂ cups boiling water

¹/₂ cup fresh lemon juice

3 cups minced fresh parsley

3 large ripe tomatoes, seeded and chopped

¹/₂ cup minced green onions

¹/₃ cup olive oil

¹/₃ cup fresh lemon juice

2 tablespoons chopped fresh mint

¹/₂ teaspoon salt

¹/₄ teaspoon pepper

Place the bulgur in a large bowl. Add the boiling water and ¹/₂ cup lemon juice; stir. Cover and let stand at room temperature for ¹/₂ hour or until the liquid has been absorbed and the bulgur is tender.

Add remaining ingredients; toss to coat. Cover and refrigerate for at least 1 hour before serving.

Makes 8 servings

TIP

Bulgur wheat is made from cooked wheat berries which have the bran removed and are then dried and crushed. It is sold by number—1 to 5—indicating the degree of coarseness, with 1 being the finest. It is readily available in Mediterranean grocery stores and in the natural food section of your local supermarket. Cracked wheat can be substituted for bulgur. Cracked wheat is made from uncooked, crushed wheat berries and retains all of the nutrients of whole wheat.

Rice Pilaf

¹/₃ **cup vermicelli**

1 **teaspoon olive oil**

1 **small onion, peeled and minced**

¹/₂ **cup butter**

2 **cups long grain rice**

4¹/₂ **cups chicken broth**

³/₄ **teaspoon salt**

¹/₄ **teaspoon pepper**

Sauté the vermicelli in the oil in a small skillet for 2 minutes or until lightly browned; set aside. Cook the onion in the butter over medium heat in a large saucepan for 3 minutes or until translucent. Add the rice; cook and stir for 1 minute. Add the chicken broth, vermicelli, salt, and pepper; stir. Bring to a boil; reduce heat. Cover and simmer for 30 to 40 minutes or until the broth is absorbed.

Makes 8 servings

Hummus

Make Hummus from the recipe on page 63 or purchase prepared hummus to serve with vegetables.

Boereg

Use the recipe on page 133 to prepare these tasty cheese triangles in advance. Store them in the refrigerator or freezer, and then bake right before serving. Leftovers can be stored in the refrigerator and reheated in the oven.

 Party Tips

Armenian Paklava is similar to the Greek Baklava, but is less sweet. Even if you've never tried to make either, they are fairly easy to make. The hardest part is working with the delicate phyllo dough.

Phyllo dough, also called fillo or strudel leaves, is usually sold frozen as a twin pack in a 16-ounce package. Depending on the manufacturer, each package will contain anywhere from 20 to 30 sheets. The size of the sheets can vary, as well. This recipe is based on 13x17-inch sheets. Check the package before you buy it so that you know what size sheets it contains.

Paklava

- 3 cups unsalted butter, clarified
- 4 cups finely chopped walnuts
- 2 teaspoons cinnamon
- 1/2 cup sugar
- 2 (16-ounce) packages phyllo dough (13x17-inch sheets), thawed
- 2 cups sugar
- 1 1/2 cups water
- 1 tablespoon fresh lemon juice

Preheat the oven to 300°F. Brush some of the melted butter on the bottom of a 12x16x1-inch baking pan.

Mix the walnuts, cinnamon, and sugar in a small bowl.

Remove the phyllo dough from the wrapper; unfold and cover with a damp dish towel. Keep the sheets covered with the damp towel while you are working so they don't dry out. Working with 1 sheet of dough at a time, carefully place the sheets in the prepared pan, brushing every other sheet with melted butter. Layer half of the dough, and then sprinkle with the walnut mixture. Continue layering the dough, this time brushing every sheet with butter, being sure to butter the top sheet. With a sharp knife, cut the pastry into diamond shapes. Bake for 1 hour or until top is lightly browned. Cool to room temperature.

Meanwhile, combine the sugar, water, and lemon juice in a saucepan. Cook over medium heat, stirring constantly, until the sugar is dissolved. Bring to a boil; cook for 10 minutes. Remove from heat; cool to room temperature.

Drizzle the syrup over the pastry diamonds, making sure that it drips down into the cut rows.

Makes 50 to 60 pieces

TIPS

To clarify the butter, bring it to a simmer over low heat in a heavy saucepan until the solids separate from the fat, about 10 to 15 minutes. Remove from heat; let stand for 5 minutes. Skim off the foam. Slowly pour off the clear yellow liquid into a small bowl through a fine strainer to remove any milk solids that may have settled to the bottom of the pan. Discard the milk solids.

Store paklava in an airtight container for up to 1 month or in the freezer for up to 2 months.

Picnic Basket

Classic chicken salad paired with tasty vegetable side salads
makes a summer outing fun and delicious.

Creamy Chicken Salad

Make the Creamy Chicken Salad on page 10, doubling the recipe and omitting the pineapple garnish.

Artichoke and Bean Salad

3 cups green beans, trimmed and cut into 2-inch pieces

$^1/_3$ cup balsamic vinegar

$^1/_4$ cup chopped fresh parsley

$^1/_4$ cup chopped fresh basil

2 tablespoons chopped fresh dill

3 tablespoons olive oil

$^1/_4$ teaspoon salt

$^1/_4$ teaspoon pepper

$1^1/_2$ cups carrot strips (2x$^1/_4$-inch)

1 (15-ounce) can chickpeas or garbanzo beans, drained

1 (15-ounce) can kidney beans, rinsed and drained

1 (14-ounce) can artichoke hearts, drained and coarsely chopped

Place the green beans in the steamer basket of a medium saucepan over 1 inch of water; bring to a boil. Cover and steam for 4 minutes or until crisp-tender; drain and rinse with cold water.

Whisk together the vinegar, parsley, basil, dill, oil, salt, and pepper in a large bowl. Add the green beans, carrots, chickpeas, kidney beans, and artichoke hearts; toss to coat. Serve chilled or at room temperature.

Makes 8 servings

TIP

Instead of cutting carrot strips, use shredded carrots, which you can purchase in the produce section of your local supermarket.

Menu

Serves 8

Creamy Chicken Salad (*See recipe on page 10*)
Artichoke and Bean Salad
Broccoli Salad
Red Potato Pea Salad
Peanut Butter Marbled Brownies

Broccoli Salad

1 ½ **pounds broccoli, cut into small florets**

1 **pound bacon, cooked and crumbled**

¼ **cup chopped red onion**

1 **cup mayonnaise**

2 **tablespoons white vinegar**

¼ **cup sugar**

Combine the broccoli, bacon, and onion in a large bowl. Mix the mayonnaise, vinegar, and sugar together. Pour the dressing over the broccoli mixture; toss to coat. Cover and refrigerate for at least 8 hours before serving.

Makes 6 servings

 Party Tips

Wherever your picnic takes place, pack paper plates, plastic ware, paper napkins, and moist towelettes for an easy cleanup.

Be sure to keep the chicken, broccoli, and potato salads chilled in a cooler until serving.

Red Potato Pea Salad

3 pounds red potatoes

1 (16-ounce) package frozen peas, thawed

1/4 cup chopped onion

1/4 cup fresh chopped parsley

2 tablespoons fresh chopped basil

1 cup plain yogurt

1/3 cup mayonnaise

2 tablespoons fresh lemon juice

2 teaspoons dried dill

1/2 teaspoon sugar

1/2 teaspoon salt

1/4 teaspoon garlic powder

1/4 teaspoon pepper

Place the potatoes in a large saucepan and cover with water by 1 inch. Bring to a boil over medium heat and cook for 15 to 20 minutes or until tender; drain and set aside to cool.

Thinly slice the cooled potatoes, leaving the skins on; place in a large bowl. Add the peas, onion, parsley, and basil; toss to combine.

Combine the yogurt, mayonnaise, lemon juice, dill, sugar, salt, garlic powder, and pepper in a small bowl. Pour the dressing over the potato mixture; mix gently. Cover and refrigerate for at least 4 hours before serving.

Makes 8 servings

TIP

Don't worry if some of the skins come off the potatoes while being sliced. You also can slice the potatoes before cooking. If you do, reduce the cooking time to 6 to 8 minutes.

Peanut Butter Marbled Brownies

1 (8-ounce) package cream cheese, softened

1 cup peanut butter

1/4 cup sugar

1 egg

1/4 cup milk

1 cup butter, softened

2 cups sugar

3 eggs

2 teaspoons vanilla extract

1 1/4 cups flour

3/4 cup unsweetened cocoa

1/2 teaspoon baking powder

1/4 teaspoon salt

Preheat the oven to 350°F. Spray a 13x9x2-inch baking pan with cooking spray.

In a large mixing bowl, beat the cream cheese, peanut butter, 1/4 cup sugar, 1 egg, and milk until smooth; set aside.

In another large mixing bowl, beat the butter and 2 cups sugar until well blended. Add the 3 eggs, one at a time, beating well after each addition. Add the vanilla; mix well. Combine the flour, cocoa, baking powder, and salt in a medium bowl. Add the flour mixture to the butter mixture; stir until combined. Remove 1 cup of the batter; set aside. Spread the remaining batter in the bottom of the prepared pan. Spread the peanut butter mixture over the batter. Drop the reserved batter by teaspoonfuls over the peanut butter mixture. Using a knife, gently swirl the batter to create a marbled affect. Bake for 45 to 50 minutes or until a wooden pick inserted into the center comes out clean. Cool completely in the pan on a wire rack. Cut into 24 squares.

Makes 24 bars

Potluck Salad Party

*Your guests can participate in putting this meal together—
give them the recipes for these easy-to-prepare dishes
as their potluck "assignments."*

Seafood Pasta Salad

Assign the centerpiece of the meal, the Seafood Pasta Salad on page 92, to yourself and make
the presentation extra-special.

Apricot Gelatin Salad

2 (6-ounce) packages dried
   apricots

2 cups water

3 (6-ounce) packages orange
   gelatin

1 (8-ounce) package cream
   cheese, softened

1 cup sour cream

1/4 cup sugar

1/2 cup chopped toasted walnuts
   or pecans

Combine the apricots and water in a saucepan; bring to a
boil. Reduce heat and simmer for 15 minutes or until the
apricots are tender. Drain the apricots, reserving the cooking
liquid.

Prepare the gelatin according to package directions, using the
reserved apricot cooking liquid for part of the water. Pour the
gelatin into a 13x9x2-inch baking dish. Refrigerate until
partly thickened.

Meanwhile, purée the apricots in a food processor. Add the
puréed apricots to the partly thickened gelatin. Refrigerate
until firm.

Beat the cream cheese, sour cream, and sugar in a medium
bowl with an electric mixer at high speed until well blended;
spread over the gelatin. Sprinkle with the nuts. Cover and
refrigerate for at least 2 hours before serving.

Makes 12 servings

Party Tip

*Purchase fresh vegetables and dill dip or Brie cheese and crackers
to serve as an appetizer.*

Menu

Serves 8

Strawberry Spinach Salad

- $1/4$ cup red wine vinegar
- $1/4$ cup extra-virgin olive oil
- 4 teaspoons sugar
- 16 cups torn fresh spinach (2 bunches)
- 2 cups sliced strawberries
- 1 cup sliced almonds
- $2/3$ cup crumbled blue cheese

Whisk together the vinegar, oil, and sugar in a small bowl. Combine the spinach, strawberries, and almonds in a large salad bowl. Drizzle the salad with the dressing; toss to coat. Sprinkle with the blue cheese.

Makes 8 servings

 ## Party Tips

Serve wine spritzers before the meal. Simply mix 6 ounces chardonnay or any dry white wine with 2 ounces of club soda; garnish with a lemon wedge or twist.

Serve a different chardonnay or white wine with the meal.

Sweet Potato Muffins

2 cups flour

$^1\!/_2$ cup light brown sugar

2 teaspoons baking powder

1 teaspoon cinnamon

$^1\!/_2$ teaspoon ground nutmeg

$^1\!/_4$ teaspoon salt

1 cup cooked and mashed
   sweet potato

$^1\!/_3$ cup milk

1 egg

$^1\!/_4$ cup butter, melted

Preheat the oven to 375°F. Spray muffin cups with cooking spray.

Combine the flour, brown sugar, baking powder, cinnamon, nutmeg, and salt in a large bowl. Stir together the sweet potato, milk, egg, and butter in a large bowl with an electric mixer at medium speed until blended. Gradually add the flour mixture to the sweet potato mixture, beating at low speed just until combined. Spoon the batter into the prepared muffin cups. Bake for 15 minutes or until a wooden pick inserted into the center comes out clean. Cool in the pan on a wire rack for 5 minutes. Remove the muffins from the pan.

Makes 12 muffins

TIP

To cook a large sweet potato quickly, place it on a microwave-safe dish. Microwave on HIGH for 10 to 15 minutes or until tender. Remove the skin and mash.

Chocolate Marshmallow Tart

2 cups graham cracker crumbs

2 tablespoons sugar

5 tablespoons butter, melted

10 ounces semisweet baking chocolate, chopped

1 ³/₄ cups heavy cream

2 cups miniature marshmallows

4 ounces semisweet baking chocolate, chopped

1 cup chopped pecans

Preheat the oven to 350°F. Spray a 9-inch tart pan with a removable bottom with cooking spray.

Combine the graham cracker crumbs, sugar, and butter in a medium bowl. Toss with a fork until the crumbs are moistened. Press onto the bottom and side of the prepared pan. Bake for 15 minutes; cool completely on a wire rack.

Place 10 ounces chopped chocolate in a medium bowl. Bring the cream to a simmer in a heavy, medium saucepan over medium-high heat. Pour the cream over the chocolate. Whisk until the chocolate is melted and smooth; set aside.

Combine the marshmallows, 4 ounces chopped chocolate, and pecans in a medium bowl. Remove ¹/₃ of the marshmallow mixture; set aside. Spread the remaining marshmallow mixture over the crust.

Remove 1 cup of the cream mixture; cover and let stand at room temperature. Pour the remaining cream mixture over the tart. Refrigerate the tart for 1 hour or until chocolate is set. Sprinkle with the remaining marshmallow mixture. Drizzle with the reserved cream mixture. Cover and refrigerate until ready to serve.

Makes 12 servings

Summer Barbecue

The pleasures of summer—luscious fruits and vegetables and warm evenings—mean that it's time to gather friends and family for a barbecue.

Hot Dogs and Hamburgers

Fire up the grill and cook hot dogs and hamburgers. Serve with all of the usual condiments, along with pickles, lettuce, and sliced tomatoes.

Fresh Corn Salad

  8 **cups fresh corn kernels (about 8 ears)**

1 1/2 **cups chopped red pepper**

1 1/4 **cups chopped onion**

  1 **teaspoon minced garlic**

  3 **tablespoons olive oil, divided**

 1/2 **cup fresh lime juice**

  2 **teaspoons sugar**

  1 **teaspoon salt**

 1/2 **teaspoon black pepper**

 2/3 **cup chopped fresh cilantro**

Cook the corn, pepper, onion, and garlic in 2 tablespoons oil in a large stockpot over medium-high heat for 8 to 10 minutes or until the onion is translucent. Remove from heat; pour into a large serving bowl and let cool.

Whisk together 1 tablespoon oil, lime juice, sugar, salt, and black pepper in a small bowl. Add the cilantro and mix well. Pour the dressing over the corn mixture and mix well. Cover and refrigerate for at least 4 hours before serving.

Makes 10 servings

 ## Party Tips

Serve potato chips and a vegetable platter with dip, if you desire.

Be sure to break out the paper plates and plastic ware to cut down on the cleanup.

Menu

Serves 10 to 12

Hot Dogs and Hamburgers
Fresh Corn Salad
Fruit Salad
Potato Salad
Peanut Butter Cookies

Fruit Salad

- 3 cups halved green grapes
- 3 cups cubed watermelon
- 2 cups sliced fresh strawberries
- 2 cups fresh blueberries
- 3 kiwifruit, peeled and sliced
- 2 Granny Smith apples, peeled, cored, and chopped
- 1/3 cup honey
- 1/3 cup frozen limeade concentrate, thawed
- 1 teaspoon sugar
- 1 cup slivered almonds

Combine the fruits in a large bowl. Whisk together the honey, limeade concentrate, and sugar in a small bowl. Pour the dressing over the fruit; toss gently to coat. Sprinkle with the almonds. Serve with a slotted spoon.

Makes 8 to 10 servings

 Party Tip

Use the remaining limeade concentrate to make a festive rum drink. Simply mix it with the following: 1 1/2 cups water, 3 cups grapefruit-flavored soda, and 3/4 cup coconut rum. You can call it your special Coconut Lime Breeze drink! It makes 5 cups. If you decide to make another batch using a full can of limeade concentrate, simply add about 1/2 cup more water and more soda and rum to taste. Enjoy!

Potato Salad

4 **pounds russet potatoes, peeled and cut into** $\frac{1}{2}$**-inch pieces**

1 **tablespoon salt**

8 **hard-cooked eggs, peeled and chopped**

1½ **cups chopped celery**

1½ **cups mayonnaise**

1 **teaspoon yellow mustard**

1 **teaspoon salt**

Place the potatoes in a large stockpot with enough water to cover by several inches. Bring to a boil over high heat; add 1 tablespoon salt. Reduce heat to medium to maintain a gentle boil. Cook for 8 minutes or until potatoes are tender when pierced with a knife; drain. Place in a large bowl and cool to room temperature. Add the eggs and celery; toss gently to mix. Combine the mayonnaise, mustard, and salt in a small bowl. Add the dressing to the potato mixture; toss gently to coat. Cover and refrigerate for at least 4 hours before serving.

Makes 10 to 12 servings

TIP

Any of the following ingredients can be added to the basic recipe above: chopped onion, chopped green pepper, chopped cornichons (small tart pickles), or chopped parsley. Increase the amount of mayonnaise in proportion to the amount of additional ingredients.

Peanut Butter Cookies

3 cups flour

1 teaspoon baking soda

1 teaspoon baking powder

¹/₄ teaspoon salt

1 cup (2 sticks) butter, softened

1 cup peanut butter

1 cup granulated sugar

1 cup packed brown sugar

2 eggs

1 teaspoon vanilla extract

¹/₃ cup granulated sugar

Preheat the oven to 375°F.

Sift together the flour, baking soda, baking powder, and salt. Beat the butter, peanut butter, 1 cup granulated sugar, and brown sugar in a large bowl with an electric mixer at high speed until fluffy. Add the eggs and vanilla; beat until blended. Gradually add the flour mixture to the peanut butter mixture, beating at low speed just until combined. Refrigerate the dough for at least 1 hour.

Pour ¹/₃ cup granulated sugar into a small bowl. Shape the dough by tablespoonfuls into 1-inch balls; roll them in the sugar. Place 2 inches apart on ungreased cookie sheets. Flatten each ball with the tines of a sugar-coated fork, making a criss-cross pattern. Bake about 10 to 12 minutes until golden. Cool on the pans for 5 minutes. Remove to wire racks; cool completely.

Makes about 4 dozen cookies

 Party Tip

Along with the cookies, serve vanilla ice cream with assorted toppings such as butterscotch, caramel, and hot fudge.

Taste of Italy Party

Fresh vegetables take center stage in this menu, which means you will have room for a fabulous dessert. Cin Cin!

Lemon Oregano Chicken Breasts

10 boneless, skinless chicken breast halves (4 to 6 ounces each)

¹/₄ cup grated lemon zest

3 tablespoons extra-virgin olive oil

5 teaspoons dried oregano

2¹/₂ teaspoons salt

1¹/₂ teaspoons coarsely ground black pepper

¹/₃ cup fresh lemon juice

¹/₃ cup minced fresh parsley

Flatten the chicken breasts to ¹/₄-inch thickness. Whisk together the lemon zest, oil, oregano, salt, and pepper in a small bowl. Rub the mixture over both sides of the flattened chicken breasts.

Prepare a medium-hot fire in a charcoal or gas grill; oil the grill grate with cooking spray.

Grill the chicken for 3 to 5 minutes a side over medium-high heat until the chicken is firm and no longer pink in the center. Remove from heat. Sprinkle with the lemon juice and parsley.

Makes 10 servings

Insalata Caprese

3 (8-ounce) packages fresh mozzarella cheese, thinly sliced

4 to 5 large ripe tomatoes, sliced

Salt and pepper, to taste

12 large fresh basil leaves, thinly sliced

¹/₄ cup extra-virgin olive oil

2 tablespoons balsamic vinegar

Additional basil leaves, as a garnish (optional)

Arrange the mozzarella and tomato slices on a platter, over-lapping them. Season with salt and pepper. Sprinkle with the basil. Whisk together the oil and vinegar in a small bowl; drizzle over the tomatoes and mozzarella cheese. Garnish with additional basil, if desired.

Makes 8 to 10 servings

TIP

Fresh mozzarella cheese is moist and soft, quick-melting, and delicate tasting. In Italy, mozzarella was originally made from water buffalo's milk. Most fresh mozzarella now comes from cow's milk, both in Italy and here in North America.

Sun-dried Tomato Pesto Torta

$^1/_2$ cup (1 stick) butter, softened

2 (8-ounce) packages cream cheese, softened

3 tablespoons prepared sun-dried tomato spread

1 (7-ounce) package prepared pesto

Fresh basil leaves, as a garnish

Toasted pine nuts, as a garnish

Italian bread, cut into $^1/_2$-inch-thick slices and toasted

Spray two 4-inch diameter springform pans with cooking spray.

Beat the butter and 1 package cream cheese in a large bowl with an electric mixer until combined. Spread $^1/_2$ cup of the cream cheese mixture in the bottom of each of the prepared pans. Remove any remaining cream cheese mixture from the bowl; reserve. In the mixing bowl, beat the remaining package of cream cheese and the sun-dried tomato spread with the electric mixer until combined.

Spread 2 tablespoons pesto over the cream cheese mixture in each of the pans. Spread with the sun-dried tomato mixture. Top with the remaining pesto and reserved cream cheese mixture. Cover and refrigerate overnight. *(Can be made up to 3 days in advance.)*

Remove torta by releasing pan sides. Place on a platter and garnish with the basil leaves and pine nuts. Serve with the toasted Italian bread slices.

Makes two 4-inch tortas

 Party Tip

Serve an assortment of Italian wines with dinner: white wines such as Pinot Grigio, Frascati, and Orvieto and red wines such as Barbaresco, Chianti, and Bardolino. For dessert, serve Marsala or Moscato.

Roasted Green Beans

2 1/2 **pounds green beans, trimmed**

   1 **tablespoon olive oil**

  1/2 **teaspoon salt**

   1 **tablespoon grated lemon zest**

   2 **tablespoons fresh lemon juice**

   2 **tablespoons extra-virgin olive oil**

  1/4 **teaspoon coarsely ground black pepper**

  1/4 **teaspoon salt**

  1/4 **cup minced fresh mint**

   2 **tablespoons chopped fresh oregano**

Preheat the oven to 450°F. Place the green beans in a large roasting pan; drizzle with 1 tablespoon olive oil. Sprinkle with 1/2 teaspoon salt; stir. Roast the green beans for 25 to 30 minutes or until tender and slightly browned, stirring twice.

In a large bowl, whisk together the lemon zest, lemon juice, 2 tablespoons extra-virgin olive oil, pepper, and 1/4 teaspoon salt until smooth. Add the green beans, mint, and oregano; toss to coat.

Makes 8 to 10 servings

 ## Party Tip

A special dessert completes this authentic Italian menu. Zuppa Inglese literally translates to "English soup"— even though it obviously isn't soupy! One theory maintains that this signature southern Italian dessert was so named because it closely resembles an English trifle. Like a trifle, Zuppa Inglese is at its best when it is made in stages. Prepare the pastry cream a day ahead. Assemble the trifle, except for the whipped cream, the morning of the day it is served. Add the whipped cream just before serving.

Zuppa Inglese

Pastry Cream

- 4 cups whole milk
- 1 cup plus 6 tablespoons sugar, divided
- 10 egg yolks
- 2/3 cup flour
- 3 ounces semisweet chocolate, chopped
- 1/2 teaspoon cinnamon
- 2 teaspoons vanilla extract
- Grated zest of 1 orange

Syrup

- 3/4 cup water
- 1/2 cup sugar
- 6 tablespoons orange-flavored liqueur (such as Grand Marnier)
- 1 (16-ounce) frozen pound cake, thawed
- 2 cups heavy cream
- 3 tablespoons sugar
- 2 teaspoons orange extract
- Chocolate shavings, as a garnish (optional)

To make the pastry cream: Bring the milk and 1/3 cup plus 3 tablespoons sugar to a simmer in a heavy, large saucepan over medium heat. Remove from heat. Meanwhile, whisk together the egg yolks and remaining 1/3 cup plus 3 tablespoons sugar in a large bowl about 3 minutes, until the mixture thickens and turns pale yellow. Add the flour; whisk until combined. Pour the hot milk into the egg mixture, whisking to combine. Pour the mixture back into the saucepan. Cook, whisking constantly, over medium heat about 3 minutes or until the pudding thickens and comes to a boil. Remove from the heat. Divide the pudding evenly between 2 bowls. Add the chocolate and cinnamon to one bowl; whisk until completely melted and the pudding is smooth. Add the vanilla and orange peel to the second bowl; stir to combine. Cover each bowl with plastic wrap, gently pressing it directly onto the surface of the pudding. Refrigerate for at least 4 hours before serving.

To make the syrup: Combine the water and sugar in a small saucepan. Cook over medium heat, stirring constantly, until the sugar is dissolved. Bring to a boil. Remove from heat; cool to room temperature. Add the liqueur; stir to combine.

To assemble: Cut the cake into 3/8-inch-thick slices; cut each slice into thirds. Cover the bottom of a 3-quart trifle dish or straight-sided glass bowl with a layer of cake pieces; brush with the syrup. Spread half of the orange pudding over the cake, all the way to the side of the bowl. Add another layer of cake pieces; brush with syrup. Spread half of the chocolate pudding over the cake, all the way to the side of the bowl. Repeat layers, ending with cake pieces brushed with syrup as the top layer. Cover and refrigerate for 4 to 8 hours before serving.

Just before serving, beat the cream in a large bowl with an electric mixer until soft peaks form. Add the sugar and orange extract; beat until stiff peaks form. Spread over the dessert. Garnish with chocolate shavings, if desired.

Makes 16 servings

Weekend Brunch

Succulent glazed ham and creamy quiche paired with two side salads, biscuits, and lemon cake create a special brunch for any weekend of the year.

Glazed Ham

Purchase a precooked, pre-sliced 8-pound ham and heat it according to the package directions. Many brands include a brown sugar glaze packet with the ham.

Buttermilk Biscuits

Serve piping hot Buttermilk Biscuits made from the recipe on page 35.

Apple Salad

2 **cups diced unpeeled Granny Smith apple**

1 **cup diced unpeeled McIntosh apple**

1 **cup diced celery**

1 **cup chopped toasted walnuts**

1 **tablespoon fresh lemon juice**

¹/₂ **cup mayonnaise**

2 **tablespoons chopped fresh flat-leaf parsley**

Mix the apples, celery, and walnuts in a large bowl; sprinkle with the lemon juice. Add the mayonnaise and parsley; stir to combine. Cover and refrigerate until serving.

Makes 8 to 10 servings

Menu	Glazed Ham
Serves 10	*Buttermilk Biscuits* (See recipe on page 35)
	Apple Salad
	Spinach Salad
	Broccoli and Swiss Cheese Quiche
	Lemon-Glazed Cake

Spinach Salad

- 8 **cups torn spinach leaves**
- 4 **hard-cooked eggs, peeled and chopped**
- ¹/₄ **cup minced red onion**
- 6 **slices bacon, cut into small pieces**
- 2 **teaspoons cornstarch**
- ¹/₃ **cup cider vinegar**
- ²/₃ **cup water**
- 1 **egg, lightly beaten**
- 2 **teaspoons sugar**
- ¹/₂ **teaspoon salt**
- ¹/₄ **teaspoon pepper**

Combine spinach, eggs, and onion in a large salad bowl. Cook the bacon in a skillet until crisp; remove with a slotted spoon and drain. Discard all but 2 tablespoons drippings. Mix together the cornstarch and vinegar in a small bowl; add the water, egg, sugar, salt, and pepper. Combine well. Stir the vinegar mixture into the drippings in the skillet. Bring to a boil over medium heat, stirring constantly. Cook for 2 minutes. Remove from heat; pour the dressing over the salad. Add the bacon; toss to coat. Serve immediately.

Makes 8 to 10 servings

TIP

For perfect hard-cooked eggs, cover the eggs with cold water by about 1 inch in a large saucepan. Heat the water, uncovered, watching for the first large bubbles to rise to the surface. Reduce heat to keep the water just below the boiling point. Cook for 10 minutes. At 10 minutes, remove one egg and quickly shell it under cold running water. Slice the egg into halves; check the yolk. If the yolk is cooked through, remove the remaining eggs from the pan. If not, cook the eggs a minute or two longer. Carefully drain the hot water and place the pan in the sink under cold running water. When the eggs are cool enough to handle, peel the eggs and refrigerate until cooled.

Broccoli and Swiss Cheese Quiche

Crust

- 2 cups sifted flour
- 1 teaspoon salt
- 1/3 cup shortening, cold
- 1/3 cup butter, cold and cut into small pieces
- 5 to 7 tablespoons ice water, divided

Filling

- 2 cups broccoli florets
- 6 eggs
- 2 cups light cream
- 1/2 teaspoon salt
- 1/4 teaspoon ground nutmeg
- 2 cups shredded Swiss cheese

To make the crust: Combine the flour and salt in a large bowl. Cut in the shortening with a pastry blender or 2 knives until the mixture resembles coarse crumbs. Cut in the butter until the pieces become the size of small peas. Sprinkle 4 tablespoons water over the flour mixture; gently toss with a fork. Add enough of the remaining water, 1 tablespoon at a time, tossing until all the flour is moistened. Gather the dough into a ball; flatten each into a disk. Wrap in plastic wrap; refrigerate for at least 1 hour. *(Pastry dough can be refrigerated for up to 3 days. Let the dough stand at room temperature to soften slightly before rolling.)*

Roll out the dough to a 14-inch round on a lightly floured surface. (The dough should be about 1/8 inch thick.) Transfer to an 11-inch quiche dish. Trim any excess dough to within 1/4 inch of the edge of the dish; press the dough over top edge of the dish. Cover the pastry crust loosely with plastic wrap. Refrigerate for at least 1 hour or up to 24 hours.

Preheat the oven to 400°F. Place the crust on a baking sheet; prick the bottom all over with a fork. Bake for 10 minutes.

To make the filling: Place the broccoli in the steamer basket of a medium saucepan over 1 inch of water; bring to a boil. Cover and steam for 5 to 8 minutes or until crisp-tender; drain and rinse with cold water. Beat the eggs, cream, salt, and nutmeg in a large bowl with an electric mixer at medium speed until well blended. Stir in the broccoli and cheese; pour into the crust. Bake for 10 minutes. *Reduce oven temperature to 325°.* Continue baking for 45 to 50 minutes or until golden brown and a wooden pick inserted into the center comes out clean. Let stand 10 minutes before cutting. *(Can be made 1 day in advance. Reheat in a 300°F oven for 15 to 20 minutes or until warm.)*

Makes 10 servings

Lemon-Glazed Cake

Cake

   3 cups flour, sifted

¹/₂ teaspoon baking soda

¹/₂ teaspoon salt

   2 cups sugar

   1 cup (2 sticks) butter, softened

   3 eggs

   1 cup milk

   Grated zest of 3 lemons

   2 tablespoons fresh lemon juice

Glaze

   2 cups confectioners' sugar, sifted

¹/₂ cup (1 stick) butter, softened

   Grated zest of 3 lemons

¹/₂ cup fresh lemon juice

Preheat the oven to 325°F. Spray a 10-inch tube pan with cooking spray.

To make the cake: Sift together the flour, baking soda, and salt; set aside. Beat the sugar and butter in a large bowl with an electric mixer at high speed until fluffy. Add the eggs one at a time, beating well after each addition. Add the flour mixture alternately with the milk, beating at medium speed after each addition. Beat in the lemon zest and lemon juice at low speed. Pour into the prepared pan, spreading evenly.

Bake for 1 hour or until a wooden pick inserted into the center of the cake comes out clean. Cool in the pan for 10 minutes. Meanwhile, make the glaze.

To make the glaze: Beat the confectioners' sugar and butter in a large bowl with an electric mixer at high speed until smooth. Beat in the lemon zest and lemon juice.

Remove the cake from the pan to a wire rack. Carefully invert the cake onto a heatproof cake plate, so the top side is up. Spread the glaze over the hot cake. Cool completely.

Makes 16 servings

 Party Tip

Serve mimosas in tall stemmed glasses—simply mix champagne with orange juice.

Index

Delicious Salad Meals

Index

Index

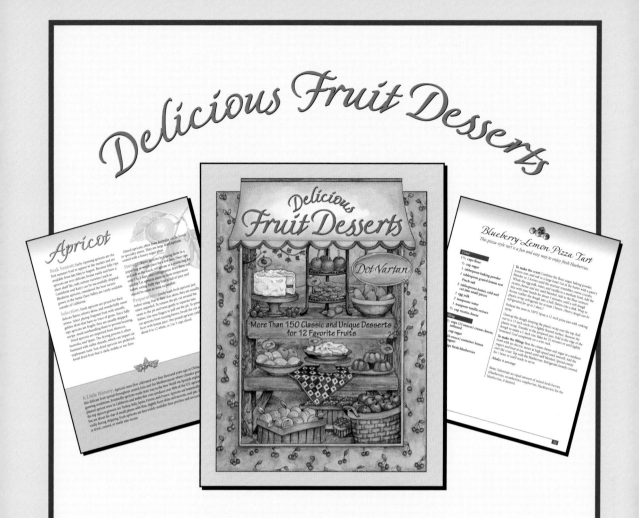

Delicious Fruit Desserts is a collection of more than 150 recipes that celebrate the bounty of orchards, groves, and fields. From apples and blueberries to cherries and peaches, twelve of the most popular fruits are showcased in an amazing array of scrumptious cookies, cakes, pies, cobblers, cheesecakes, and tarts. Each of the twelve chapters is devoted to a different fruit and includes a brief history as well as useful information on selecting, storing, and preparing nature's harvest. Fruit tips and anecdotes are also sprinkled throughout the book.

Delicious Fruit Desserts is one cookbook you'll turn to again and again for sweet endings to all of life's occasions, from weeknight dinners and potluck suppers to family celebrations and entertaining friends.